Contents

Part One: Introduction – issues and sources   5

  1.1 Sources for Roman Britain   7

  1.2 Tacitus as a source for Roman Britain   8

  1.3 Working with archaeological sources   11

  1.4 Summing up the sources   19

Part Two: Britain and Rome – conquest and culture   22

  2.1 The Roman conquest of Britain: a historical outline   22

  2.2 Britain before the Claudian conquest   26

  2.3 Britain in the post-conquest years: *civitas, colonia*
      and client kingdoms   32

Part Three: The army and Roman Britain   42

  3.1 Serving emperor and empire   42

  3.2 The identity of the Romano-British soldier   49

  3.3 Frontier culture: military and civilian in northern Britain   60

Part Four: Presenting Roman Britain   71

  4.1 Event, image and ideology   71

  4.2 Images of Boudicca   73

  4.3 Images of Boadicea   78

  4.4 Presenting the past: 'fact' and 'fiction'   80

Conclusion to Block Four   87

Key dates   88

References   89

Further reading   90

KU-042-201

The Open University

AA309 B4
Arts: Level 3

CULTURE, IDENTITY AND POWER IN THE ROMAN EMPIRE

BLOCK FOUR
Roman Britain

Prepared for the Course Team by Janet Huskinson (Block Convenor),
Valerie Hope and Lisa Nevett

The Open University
Walton Hall, Milton Keynes MK7 6AA

First published 2000. Reprinted 2002

Copyright © 2000 The Open University

All rights reserved. No part of this publication may be reproduced, stored in a retrieval system, transmitted or utilized in any form or by any means, electronic, mechanical, photocopying, recording or otherwise, without written permission from the publisher or a licence from the Copyright Licensing Agency Ltd. Details of such licences (for reprographic reproduction) may be obtained from the Copyright Licensing Agency Ltd of 90 Tottenham Court Road, London W1P 0LP.

Edited, designed and typeset by The Open University

Printed and bound in the United Kingdom by the Alden Group, Oxford

This text is a component of the Open University course AA309 *Culture, Identity and Power in the Roman Empire*. Details of this and other Open University courses can be obtained from the Course Reservations Centre, PO Box 724, The Open University, Milton Keynes MK7 6ZS, United Kingdom: tel. (00 44) (0) 1908 653231, email ces-gen@open.ac.uk

For availability of this or other course components, contact Open University Worldwide Ltd, The Berrill Building, Walton Hall, Milton Keynes MK7 6AA, United Kingdom: tel. (00 44) (0) 1908 858785; fax (00 44) (0) 1908 858787; e-mail ouwenq@open.ac.uk

Alternatively, much useful course information can be obtained from the Open University website http://www.open.ac.uk

ISBN 0 7492 8773 X

24900B/aa309b4i1.2

Part One: Introduction – issues and sources

BY JANET HUSKINSON AND LISA NEVETT

So far in this course you have looked at the impact of empire in Rome and Italy and in the Greek east. These were areas where contacts between Rome and the local cultures had been well established before the advent of empire occasioned new forms and expressions of power and reappraisal of identity. In this block you will encounter a rather different situation. Britain, on the geographical periphery of the Roman world, had had more limited contacts with Rome before its eventual conquest by the emperor Claudius in AD 43; and furthermore its own cultural traditions were very different from those of Greece and Rome. Romans, in their turn, had little direct knowledge of Britain. Particularly since Julius Caesar's initial attempts at invading the island in 55 and 54 BC there had been some trade and limited travel to Britain, yet as powerful perhaps as these 'real' experiences in Roman minds was the image of Britain as a strange northern country across the ocean, with an exotically different culture. But if the desire to conquer this alien place was one motive to invade, once there the Romans had to find ways of incorporating the native people with their particular traditions into the culture of the empire.

So this is the setting for the particular issues of culture, identity and power which are examined in this block on Britain. Although Roman Britain offers wide scope for these subjects, the chosen focus for this block is on the military aspects of the conquest and on the presence of imperial power in a frontier zone. This opens up questions about the role of the Roman army and the identity of its soldiers, and about Roman strategies for maintaining control, especially through cultural developments. It looks again at processes of 'Romanization' (which you have already met, in Block Two for instance), questioning local reactions as well. To what extent was 'Roman' culture in Britain imposed or emulated, resisted or adopted? How far is it appropriate to see the situation in oppositional terms, as 'Romans versus Britons'? Such issues will be at the heart of your work in this block.

Running through the block are two other themes. One is the presentation of historical situations and how this colours our view of them. This of course is a concept fundamental to the use of any historical source. Indeed as you have been analysing the writings of different historians, you have been considering how and why they chose to write their histories as they did; and in the next block on Roman

North Africa there will be a chance to look at how the immediate past (in a colonial form) led scholars to approach archaeology in a particular way. But presentation also shapes our own reactions to the past and what we choose to believe or commemorate about it. Presentation has the power to suggest what is significant for later cultures in the heroes and heroines of the past, or in historical sites, or in the artefacts that are displayed in museums. It affects how we identify our own roles as present-day interpreters of culture in the Roman empire, and also how we look at the way in which previous generations in their turn presented the Roman past.

gender

The second is the theme of gender which recurs at various points in the block. In Essay One (which you read at the start of the course) there was discussion of the El Djem mosaic which used female personifications to depict Rome surrounded by provinces. This block further explores the way in which gender can be used to symbolize power relations through representations of Britannia (the personification of Britain) and Boudicca (whom you may also know by the later name of Boadicea).

To consider all these issues your work will concentrate on particular topics. The first part of the block will introduce you to sources for Roman Britain. The second will consider the Roman invasion of Britain and its impact on local societies during the late first and early second centuries AD. The third part will look at the Roman army, the northern frontier zone and its culture; and the final part will be on presenting the past, through an examination of the treatment of Boudicca by Roman historians and in later British art and literature, and also in present-day displays of Romano-British material in museums.

This block will comprise three weeks' study time with a further week in which to prepare your TMA. As a rough guideline, the first two parts together are about a week's work, and Parts Three and Four will take about a week each. This block has more video to watch than the other blocks have had (largely because of the higher amount of archaeological and visual material that it involves), so you may need to take this into account as you arrange your working time; there are five video sequences and two audio bands which you will be directed to at specific points during the block. You may find the two maps of Britain in Goodman pages 209 and 210 useful for background information.

For this part of the block your work will require the Offprints Book and Illustrations Book. You will also be listening to an interview on audio cassette 4, band 1, and looking at a sequence on video cassette 2, 'Archaelogy at Arbeia'.

1.1 Sources for Roman Britain

In most of the course so far the ancient sources of evidence have been plentiful and you have been able to work with both written *and* material sources, often side by side. But Britain is rather a different case. Opportunities to work with literary and material evidence together are few compared with the possibilities that exist for other parts of the empire (for Augustan Rome for instance). This means that there are sometimes crucial gaps in the evidence but this does help to set up a lively debate as scholars are constantly reassessing the evidence that is available and looking at it in the light of new lines of argument. (This in itself is a reminder that cultural identity is not a static concept but always open to reworking and reinterpretation.) Sometimes, too, archaeological discoveries are made which blow apart (or confirm) long-held theories about Romano-British society. All in all it is an exciting area in which to work.

There are indeed some important literary sources for Britain which you will encounter here, but compared with those available for the earlier blocks they are limited in type and number. Chief amongst them are the military commentaries written by Julius Caesar in the mid first century BC, and the histories written by Suetonius and Tacitus in the late first and early second centuries AD. But, as you will shortly hear in an interview about Tacitus on the audio cassette, these very much reflect a Roman agenda; there are no first-hand literary sources which record the British view. The great speeches in defence of liberty put into the mouths of British leaders such as Calgacus (by Tacitus, and discussed in Essay Ten) and Boudicca (by Cassius Dio, in a text which you will be reading later in this block) in fact articulate a Roman rhetoric of dissent from the empire, and cannot be taken as 'British' sources. So while the written sources give a view of how Britain and its inhabitants may have appeared to people writing from the centre of empire, there are no comparable literary records by Britons themselves.

On the other hand material sources are plentiful. Objects, buildings, inscriptions and visual art from different contexts provide a wide range of information about life in Britain at this time. Some are patently to do with the invading culture while others may reflect indigenous attitudes or customs.

The following sections will introduce you to some specific aspects of the sources for Roman Britain. Note how the relationship between literary sources and (material) archaeological sources is a recurrent theme in the discussions you hear on the audio cassette and in the offprints you read.

1.2   Tacitus as a source for Roman Britain

You have already met Tacitus in Block One, section 2.4. You may find it useful to reread that section briefly now, particularly for what it says about Tacitus' approach to writing history and also about his views of the emperors Domitian and Trajan.

80s AD
governor Agricola
& father-in-law of
Tacitus

Tacitus refers to Britain at various places in his *Histories* and *Annals*, but his most substantial discussion of its geography, inhabitants and history occurs in his biography of the governor Agricola who played a major role in consolidating the Roman conquest in Britain during the eighties AD. In fact Agricola was the historian's father-in-law and the *Agricola* is something of a eulogy, though for reasons to do with politics in Rome as much as family pride. We need to be aware of how this agenda from the centre of empire affects Tacitus' presentation of events in Britain at the periphery of the empire, and how – in turn – this affects the value of the account as a source material.

Exercise

cassette 4.1

Please read extract 4.1, which gives some of Tacitus' account of the Roman conquest of Britain, and then listen to the interview with David Braund on audio cassette 4, band 1, 'Tacitus on Britain'. As you listen, jot down your responses to the following questions (which represent key points in his discussion).

1   Why, according to David Braund, was Britain an attractive subject for Tacitus to write about?

2   What does he identify as three of the pressing issues of Roman politics which Tacitus addresses in his presentation of events in Britain?

3   What are the two main points he makes about using Tacitus as a source of evidence for the history of Roman Britain?

Since Braund refers to them in the interview, you may find the following points useful.

Libertas literally means 'freedom' and *servitium*, 'servitude', but both are used by Tacitus with strong political overtones. *Libertas* 'was the watchword of those planning to restore the republic, and embodied the power of the old senatorial stratum who had run Rome' (James, Essay Ten, p.281), while *servitium* was used to signify the deprivation of freedom under a tyrannical emperor.

Caesar (Gaius Julius Caesar, 102–44 BC) wrote a commentary on his campaigns in Gaul (when he had attempted to invade Britain in 55–54 BC), *The Gallic War.* Book 5 includes a description of Britain and its peoples.

Pomponius Mela wrote a geographical survey of the inhabited world in around AD 40. He describes Britain in the third book of this, along with other places on the periphery of the Mediterranean world.

The tomb of Classicianus, set up in London, is now in the British Museum (see Figure 4.1; you will meet it again in video cassette 2, sequence 5, 'Presenting Roman Britain'). Its fragmentary inscription translates: 'To the spirits of the departed of Gaius Julius Alpinus Classicianus, son of Gaius, of the Fabian voting-tribe. Procurator of the Province of Britain, Julia Pacata I ... daughter of Indus ... his wife, set this up.'

Figure 4.1 *The tomb of Classicianus, British Museum London. (© The British Museum)*

T, explicitly says: Interest Put own private interests at head of public + tried to undermine gov. Petillinus quite disgracefully. No inkling of class having any interest at all in protecting the Britons.

political
Agricola
T's aim minimize
Dom's successes.
Agricola's achievement.

conquest - desire
for knowledge
Britain 'exotic'

Roman domestic
politics played out
elsewhere.

3 main issues pol. concern
in dome played out by T
+ in presentation of events
in Britain.
Libertas / servitium
women power
slaves / freedmen

Tacitus

don't pluck out
excerpts from T as
evidence re Britain
full context imp't

Discussion

1   Braund gives two rather different reasons as to why Britain was an attractive subject for Tacitus. The first is political, namely that events in Britain, and particularly the career of Agricola as its governor, give Tacitus scope to 'rewrite the history of the emperor Domitian's imperial successes' in order to minimize them. It allows him to show how the conquest of Britain was secured through the leadership of Agricola, rather than that of Domitian. The second reason is to do with Roman curiosity about an unknown and supposedly exotic country that lay across the ocean. Notice how Braund links this to a whole raft of questions to do with conquest and desire for knowledge, exploration as a justification for imperialist enterprises, civilization and barbarity. Indeed many Roman writers of the early empire used ethnographical themes in this way, as a counterfoil for the discussion of domestic politics; this is the link with the issues in the second question.

2   Braund clearly identifies three main issues of political concern in Rome which Tacitus plays out again in his presentation of events in Britain. It is important to be clear about these as they will recur later in the block, particularly when you come to work on Tacitus' account of Boudicca and the revolt of AD 60–61. First is a major theme of his historical writing, that is, the interplay between freedom (*libertas*) and servitude (*servitium*), which he takes to be linked with good and bad government. The irony he presents, via the British situation, is that Britons can display *libertas* in their supposedly uncivilized state while the Romans, despite being the conquerors, represent *servitium*. The other two issues also involve a sense of potential social subversion. They are what Braund describes as 'woman power', and the excessive power of slaves and freedmen, both of which were seen as threats to contemporary Roman society and political stability. Women acting as men were expected to do, and freedmen taking the powers of senators, represented a world that had turned upside down.

3   Braund warns against plucking out excerpts from Tacitus' writings to use as evidence for points about Britain and ignoring their context in his much wider picture of Roman politics.

This need to respect the full context is surely right and proper, but does it invalidate the use of excerpts altogether? It is certainly difficult to avoid using them from time to time. For instance, you have met quotations from *Agricola* 21 at several points in the course material so far, especially Tacitus' comments that the 'population gradually fell into the seductive vices of arcades, baths, and sumptuous banquets. This was called culture by the ignorant, while it was actually part of their enslavement' (quoted at the start of Essay Eight). My view is that while this should be understood as an ironic comment made in the context of Tacitus' wider views about contemporary Roman values, it does describe processes which were part of an actual historical situation, and so it is a valid passage to cite as evidence about Romanization.

irony/

processes

But overall, it is certainly important to be cautious in choosing and using passages from Tacitus as historical evidence, not least because his particular style of writing offers many eminently quotable aphorisms: it is very tempting to concentrate on witty sound-bites, at the risk of losing sight of the overall context.

*caution re↑
as historical
evidence*

Braund also warns against trying to link archaeology and Tacitus' literary text as a way of developing evidence. Why is this? For him, as you heard, the two offer evidence about different things and in very different ways, and these differences should be respected.

*Braund
agst linking
archeology +
T's lit. text to
dev. evidence.
Differences be
respected.*

1.3   Working with archaeological sources

This point leads on to evidence from material, or archaeological, sources which plays an important part in this block. As this is the first time in the course that your work will depend so much on material evidence, this section offers some preparation.

In considering a situation such as that of Roman Britain for which there is such limited first-hand literary evidence, archaeology plays an important part (if you want to revise what you read about this at the start of the course look back at Wells's survey on pp.40–46). Here again context is important, particularly so when many types of material evidence, such as artefacts and works of art, can be removed from their place of discovery and find their way to museum collections, for instance; or they may be used in book illustrations, again without reference to where they were found. In this section you will consider archaeological material in two specific contexts: first, in the context of arguments about the historical past, and second, in the context of a particular site, the Roman fort at South Shields. In each case context is an important factor in relating one piece of source material to another (which objects were found with what, for instance, or how they relate to fixed points of dating); and it is these interrelationships which can shed

acculturation: culture chges which occur when 2 autonomous cultures meet

assimilation: in cultural terms, making similar to features of another culture

Romanization: in basic terms the process whereby Roman culture spread to other cultures

particularly useful light on cultural relationships between communities, such as 'Romanization', acculturation and assimilation. (Check the Glossary if you want to remind yourself of these terms.)

Exercise

offprint 4.1
R F J Jones

In a moment you will be asked to read an offprint from R.F.J. Jones: *Britain in the Roman Period: Recent Trends.* As you will see, this deals with the matter of analysing archaeological source material so that it can be used effectively to provide historical evidence. In fact Jones's two case studies, burial and religious practices, also make relevant background reading for topics that you will be studying later in the block. In connection with the points Jones makes about religious practices, you may find it useful to think back to some of the material from Ephesus which you met in Block Three.

In terms of the relationship between literary and archaeological source material you will notice that Jones, too, takes up a particular position. Like Braund, he is clear that the two do have distinct and rather different spheres of reference. But he argues strongly that its archaeology should be the prime source of information about the culture of Roman Britain, and should be addressed on its own terms 'and not as a deficient written source'. Jones represents one voice in a wide debate about this issue, and you may find it useful to see how Wells (pp.45–6) describes the relationship between the two types of source material in rather more flexible terms; and you will see later in the work you will be doing in section 3.3 on the northern frontier region of Britain that there are cases where both types of source are needed together. (You may also like to consider how far Jones uses 'written' to mean 'literary' sources, overlooking perhaps non-literary written material such as inscriptions and the Vindolanda writing tablets which are not so easy to contrast with 'artefact' evidence.) Bearing these points in mind, make notes on the following questions as you read.

1   What does Jones identify as 'the central issue in the study of the Roman period in Britain'?

2   In order to use archaeology as a source of evidence 'on its own terms', what particular problems (according to Jones) need to be addressed? What approach does he suggest? (Concentrate on the first page of the extract in answering this.)

3   How does this approach work out in the case study of burial practices? What can each of the three levels suggest?

Please read offprint 4.1, 'Cultural change in Roman Britain'.

Discussion

1   Jones is quite clear that the central issue of this period is the nature of the interaction of native British and imported Roman practices. This indeed is also the central issue of this block. But given that our overall course themes are culture, identity and power, we are likely to be particularly interested in the context and consequences of the interaction as well as its nature. These elements are also implicit in some of the terms Jones uses in these first two sentences, such as 'the *intrusive* Roman empire' and 'all patterns of culture as *learned* behaviour' (my italics).

[margin note:] Central issue native > interaction native British + imported Roman purchees.

2   How we go about looking for aspects of 'identity and power' in the archaeological record is exactly the kind of problem that Jones has in mind when he sets out the difficulties and his suggested approach to them on his first page. A major difficulty presented by the abundant archaeological material is how to convert it into evidence appropriate to the kinds of questions that are being asked of it. As Jones so clearly states, it is relatively easy to chart developments in tangible artefacts such as pottery and houses, and answer questions relevant to those, but it is much harder when it comes to more abstract concepts. This is where our interests in the intangibles of culture, identity and power come into the picture: just how can we work with archaeological data to address the kinds of issues that they raise? The solution that Jones suggests is a careful categorization of material to provide three levels of approach, so that arguments can progress from the observable 'things you can excavate', to the relationships that can be made between these things, and finally reaching a stage where inferences can be drawn from the relationships.

[margin note:] abstract concepts as evidence – difficult

[margin note:] categorization of material to provide 3 levels approach observable – relationships – inferences

3   In the rest of the paper he develops this line of approach within the chosen case studies. A good illustration of what it produces is provided by the conclusion to the section on burial practices (starting in the second column, third paragraph). Here the progression is clearly demonstrated through observable variation in cultural forms (for example, through excavated grave goods), to arguments about what this might suggest of the different ways in which people defined themselves (their cultural identity, in other words), and ultimately to what this in turn can contribute to a general picture of society in Roman Britain.

[margin note:] burial practices observable – arguments – contribute

[margin note:] 3 level approach

Finally, you may like to consider how this three-level approach advocated by Jones for archaeological material relates to the 'three-stage' interrogation of source material that was suggested to you (in audio cassette 1, band 1) as a way of working with all kinds of material. By now you should have these three stages – close reading, contextualizing and evaluating – at your fingertips! Clearly Jones's three levels – observing, relating, and inferring (to give a slim-line summary) – share important elements so you should not find them hard to use. In fact we will be returning later in the block to several of the issues raised by Jones, when looking at archaeological material from the frontier area and religious art in Roman Britain (and you will be taking some of Jones's points further in Block Five, when you start to consider other, theoretical, ways of working with archaeological data).

close reading
context.
evaluation

As you have just seen, a first stage in working with archaeological sources lies in considering what Jones described as 'Cultural Forms (Things you can excavate)'. (It is worth noting at this point that excavation is not the only way of recovering such things. Another method which is often used is field survey, whereby the surface of a particular area is systematically searched under controlled conditions.)

" Cultural Forms
(things) you can excavate)

Questions need to be asked, for instance, about the nature of the objects found ('the finds'), where they were discovered individually and in relation to each other, and about how they might have got there. This is where an understanding of the features of a particular site is so crucial, and this can be built up by careful excavation and then through the meticulous recording of discoveries. Your second exercise on material sources will now look at how this is done at one specific site.

In video cassette 2, sequence 1, 'Archaeology at Arbeia', you will be looking in detail at some of the archaeological work which has been done on the site of the Roman fort at South Shields at the mouth of the river Tyne (its ancient name seems to have been Arbeia). (You will find a plan of the fort during one of its main phases of occupation, together with a more detailed plan and a reconstruction of one of the buildings, in the Illustration Book, Plates 4.1–4.3.) Arbeia is a site which you will meet again in other parts of this block as it obviously has direct relevance for studies of the Roman army in Britain and the culture of the frontier zone. But it was chosen here because it has been systematically excavated since Victorian times and has work-rooms adjacent to the site where the material is recorded, and a museum and a reconstructed Roman gateway in which the excavated material is interpreted for visitors. Arbeia is also the base of a historical re-enactment group, the so-called *cohors quinta Gallorum* ('fifth cohort of Gauls'). As well as putting on displays, this group also provides the chance for some scholarly research into the fighting methods and equipment of auxiliaries in third-century Britain.

The video sequence looks in detail at some of the ways in which the archaeological evidence from Arbeia has been used to address a variety of questions about the organization of the settlement in Roman times and about its role in relation to other Roman sites in the area. Close attention is paid to some of the processes involved in excavation and interpretation. The purpose is to give you an opportunity to consider the contribution made by different types of evidence to the overall picture archaeology provides. In particular, you will be invited to think about some of the strengths and weaknesses of the archaeological evidence and how they might affect the conclusions that can be drawn, not only about Arbeia, but also about settlements in other parts of the empire.

As you watch the video sequence, please make a note of the main factors affecting the interpretation of the different types of evidence discussed (*in situ* remains; small finds; bulk finds). You will be asked to use these afterwards as a basis for thinking about some of the more general issues.

Please watch video cassette 2, sequence 1 now (t.c.00:00–19:03).

VC 2 · 1
Arbeia
South shields

Exercise

The video illustrates a variety of the strengths and the weaknesses of the archaeological material from Arbeia, and most of the factors affecting the evidence from this site are also relevant to other Roman sites, both in Britain and in other provinces. It is important that you have an understanding of just how the nature of the archaeological evidence affects its interpretation. For this reason, building on the notes you have already made, take some time now to make further brief notes on the following questions.

- What sorts of questions can we address using the different types of evidence we have seen from Roman Arbeia? What potential difficulties are involved? You might find it helpful to focus your thoughts by starting with Plates 4.2 and 4.3 (the plan and reconstruction of barrack blocks): how strong is the evidence for the various features depicted? Remember that in this case the dotted lines on Plate 4.2 represent the lines of walls which were not found, but which the excavators consider to have been present in the buildings.

- To what extent are the same kinds of questions and problems also relevant to the interpretation of sites elsewhere in the Roman empire? (To help you, think back to the material evidence you have studied from places such as Rome, Pompeii,

Ostia, Athens and Ephesus. You might also like to think back over the reading you have done on sources of evidence generally, in the Introduction to the Course, especially on Wells.)

Discussion

Here are some of the issues you may have begun to think about. At a site such as Arbeia, where little of the architecture is preserved, the lines of the foundations for different buildings offer an opportunity to explore their shape and the organization of the space within them. By excavating systematically and paying attention to the order in which different deposits were laid down, it is possible to reconstruct some of the processes by which the different buildings were constructed, and to investigate how the use of an area changed through time. Nevertheless, poor preservation can sometimes leave even the most basic questions – such as the organization of rooms – in doubt. As the example of the barrack buildings shows, even the walls defining the different spaces within a building are not always clearly defined. This has meant that the reconstruction of many of the internal walls of the barrack blocks has had to be based on the organization of better preserved areas. It is important to keep this fact in mind, and any conclusions drawn about the internal organization of the blocks must necessarily be tentative. Even in relation to block II, which is better preserved than block III, there is more evidence for some features than for others: for example, the theoretical existence and location of the partition walls at the western end of the building are estimates based on walls at the eastern end. Furthermore, although the positions of the original doorways are marked by heavy doorsteps, the height and position of the windows is more difficult to assess where only the bases of the walls are preserved. Similarly, although terracotta tiles found during excavation showed that there was a pitched tile roof, there must have been less evidence for the height and angle of that roof.

Inside the blocks, built features such as hearths and ovens provide a clue to some of the activities which took place in different areas. This information is augmented by details of the finds, which can offer further information about the function of an area where there are objects used for a narrow range of functions, such as cooking pots. Styles of pottery may also tell us about trading patterns: amphorae, for example, may have been traded over long distances as containers for goods such as wine and olive oil, although it is important to recognize that some of these vessels may have been reused, and this would affect the precision with which they could be used for dating and might mean that they have arrived on the site via an indirect route. Pottery is also sometimes used in an effort to establish the identities of those who used it at a particular location. This is especially important in an area such as Britain, where we may want to know whether objects traded from elsewhere in the Roman world were used by individuals from other provinces or from Italy, or whether they were being used by indigenous groups. Nevertheless, it is dangerous to assume that there was a one-to-one correspondence between those who made a particular type of pottery and those who used it. In order to address this kind of question it is best to consider the context in which the objects were found and the relative quantities of finds of different types.

Bulk finds such as pottery can also give us an idea of the time at which an area was occupied, although the date these finds provide is often quite vague since many pottery shapes were in use for several centuries. More precise evidence for dating comes from small finds such as coins and lead seals. Ideally, such items can be used to date a specific layer and therefore the activities associated with it, which may include, for example, the construction of a building. As you saw at Arbeia, however, the earliest excavation was undertaken during Victorian times, when digging often proceeded more quickly than might be the case today, and when less information was recorded. As Alex Croom, the archaeologist on the video, points out, this means that although a number of lead seals are known to have come from the site, the exact locations where most of them were found are unknown (t.c.12:46). Instead of being used potentially to date a phase of activity and any buildings associated with it, these objects can now only be used to confirm that there was Roman activity on the site as a whole during a certain period. Even where the exact context for an object can be established, it is important to recognize that a find can only tell us the date *after* which an activity took place, since we do not know how much time elapsed between its manufacture and its final deposition. This problem is especially relevant to coins, which can be linked with particular emperors and sometimes with specific events, and therefore often provide quite precise dates. Nevertheless it is important to be aware that the coins themselves may have been in circulation for some time, and they therefore provide what is known as a *terminus post quem* ('time after which') for a particular stratigraphic level. Small finds can be used to address specific questions relating to the occupants of a site: for example the painted Cupid shown in the video (t.c.12:05) points to the high status of the occupant of the building in which it was found, since such decoration is rare. It also invites parallels with the decoration of the domestic buildings you saw in Block Three, suggesting that an effort was being made to re-create an environment which recalled Roman housing elsewhere in the empire.

In the context of Arbeia, then, the archaeological material is obviously of prime importance because it informs us about a site for which very little textual evidence remains: archaeology is almost the only means of exploring the settlement history of South Shields and its role in the context of the region as a whole. Nevertheless, archaeology also has an important role to play even in the context of major cities such as Rome and Ephesus, where more extensive textual evidence is available about the nature of Roman activity. At such sites, archaeology can contribute in two main ways. First, it can provide corroboration of information gleaned from textual sources, and secondly and more importantly, it can enable us to explore issues which appear rarely, if ever, in texts. For example, we would know almost nothing about the private lives of the residents of Ephesus if it were not for the excavated remains of their houses, which you saw in Block Three. Archaeology also provides direct evidence of past activity, in contrast with other forms of evidence, which are filtered by human choice as well as the chances involved in preservation. Literary texts, for instance, address topics selected for discussion by, and view the world from the perspective of, individual authors. (An example of this, again from Block Three, is Juvenal's third *Satire*, in which a particular slant is taken for comic effect.) Even inscriptions, although often recording a specific act or event (such as an individual's death or the donation of money) are calculated to create a particular impression.

So, archaeological evidence is important in the context of some of the big urban sites you have studied in previous blocks, although it may play a slightly different role because of the availability of other sources of evidence. The reliability of archaeological evidence in these contexts is also affected by some of the factors you have been thinking about in relation to Arbeia. Again, the preservation of individual buildings or monuments governs the specific questions that can be asked and the reliability of the conclusions that can be drawn from them. Many of the areas that you have studied in previous blocks include buildings in much more durable material than those at Arbeia, with the result that many of those buildings are much more complete. As you have seen, where details such as architectural features are preserved, they enable issues such as stylistic affiliation to be explored so that more specific questions can be asked, for example, about the cultural affiliations of those who constructed them. Paradoxically, however, problems such as construction methods and the phasing of buildings are sometimes more difficult to resolve at these well-preserved sites, since there can be a reluctance to remove walls and floors to investigate construction elements such as foundation trenches, and to look for previous phases.

It is also sometimes the case that well-preserved buildings are excavated primarily out of an interest in their architecture. Although small finds are often preserved because they help to date the construction and use of a structure and/or because they have intrinsic value, there has been a tendency in the past to ignore the majority of the bulk finds, and this has meant that it has been hard to address some of the questions raised above, such as those relating to the use of particular structures or rooms.

In sum, archaeological evidence enables a variety of questions to be addressed which relate to the date at which an area was occupied, what it may have looked like, the way it was used, and sometimes also the identities of those who frequented it. Nevertheless, archaeological evidence raises its own problems, and you need to be aware of them when you make use of this kind of information. Difficulties can arise from the way in which the material is collected and interpreted: one of the key points emerging from the various interviews – and from the discussion above – is the interconnected character of the evidence. This generally means that the more information we have, the more secure and detailed a reconstruction can be made of the history of the site. Conversely, where less information is available, the conclusions drawn should be more general, and sometimes more tentative.

1.4   Summing up the sources

To consolidate some central points that have been made in this Introduction, please look at the sculpted panel shown in Plate 4.4 in the Illustrations Book. The panel was discovered in 1980 and is an image which is often used now as an illustration in books on Roman Britain (such as Salway, 1993, p.50; Crummy, 1997, p.32 and James and Rigby, 1997, Figure 4). It comes, in fact, not from Britain but from Aphrodisias in south-western Turkey, from a sanctuary erected for the imperial cult in the mid first century AD. The building was decorated with an extensive programme of sculptures, including images of various Roman emperors (Smith, 1987 and 1988); and a Greek inscription

[handwritten margin note: Britannia / personification / Britford]

(Plate 4.5) found near this panel reveals that these figures are 'Tiberius Claudius Caesar' (that is, the emperor Claudius) and 'Bretannia'. This identification with the emperor Claudius may be confirmed by comparing the man's hair and facial features (idealized though they are) with recognized portraits of the emperor Claudius (see, for example, Figure 9.6 in Essay Nine: note the same arrangement of hair and the broad brow). The personification of Britain is in fact the earliest known so far.

So here, then, is a representation of the emperor Claudius and Britain, from a context which celebrated the achievements of Roman emperors. But what does it show of the themes of culture, identity and power that are relevant to this block?

Exercise

Note down briefly what you see in these two figures: their positions, body language and dress. What seems to be happening between them? What particular aspects of 'culture, identity and power' are suggested by the image? (You may find it useful to look back at the exercise you did in the Introduction to the Course (pp.13–14), on the soldier's tombstone.)

Discussion

[handwritten margin note: Britannia + Claudius]

The emperor is shown like a warrior, but in rather an heroic style as he wears only a cloak apart from a helmet and baldric (remember the heroic nudity of the general mentioned on audio cassette 1, band 3 in the talk on Portraiture, illustrated in Plate 2.42) and his facial features are individual yet idealized. He is equipped with a scabbard and shield and probably held a spear in his right hand which is now destroyed. Britannia, slumped at his feet, is dressed in a short tunic which leaves one breast exposed; her long hair hangs loose and she wears a broad bracelet. Their body language indicates some violent interaction: it seems that he has overpowered her to the very point of rape or even death. He holds her down with his knee and raises his spear as if for the final blow; she in turn lifts her right hand as if to resist or beg for mercy. Despite their rather impassive faces we are left in no doubt, I think, that this is an act of force and subjection.

Bearing in mind some of the imagery discussed in Essay One and in the Introduction to the Course, we can see that the way in which Claudius and Britannia are represented here sets up a particular view of their respective identities and of their relationship. For instance, the sculpture draws on styles and forms of classical Greek art and uses some common conventions of gesture and dress to signal important information about the figures. As you saw, the emperor is clearly shown as a warrior, while Britannia's unbound hair and bracelet indicate that she is some kind of 'barbarian' (since Greek and Roman women would have their hair pinned up) and other 'coded' signs from their dress – his near-nudity and her tunic which resembles the dress of classical huntresses or fighters – suggest that viewers were meant to place the figures in the world of classical heroism. So the image conveys some strong messages about identity, and an unmistakeable one about power. The arrangement of the figures shows the emperor as victor and Britannia as victim, and this inequality of power is restated in gendered terms (to recall another block theme), by showing an active male and submissive female.

The scene itself contrasts the cultural identities of classical hero and barbarian adversary, and in its own context shows a further mix of Greek and Roman elements. The sanctuary complex in Aphrodisias, from which it comes, was decorated with a series of figured reliefs which show an interesting mixture of Greek traditions of representation (myth and allegory for example) with subjects from Roman imperial history (including Augustus and Nero with 'conquests') (Smith, 1987). This is particularly clear in this image of Claudius' conquest where the very poses of the figures recall famous Greek representations of the hero Achilles killing the Amazon Penthesileia; this is in sharp contrast to the message promoted by the imperial art designed at Rome where emperors were usually shown sparing the conquered. So the scene presents the power relationship using various cultural references, yet with a single focus: imperial power is shown as heroic, invincible and overwhelming.

But how far does this image tie in with the picture presented by other ancient sources for a study of Britain? The sculpture seems to present the experience of Rome's conquest of Britain in oppositional terms: on one side there is the classical Graeco-Roman hero, on the other the apparent victim of physical force facing possible extinction. There seems no room for negotiation or compromise. Were the real historical positions – Roman and British – actually so clear cut ? Or was there room on each side for adaptation and a future life together? Your work in the next two parts of this block is centred on this enquiry, examining various forms of evidence.

Part Two: Britain and Rome – conquest and culture

BY JANET HUSKINSON

This part of the block will look at relations between Britain and Rome up to the revolt led by Boudicca in AD 60–61 (although some of the material, such as the passage from Goodman that you will read, will be central to your understanding of the block as a whole). The aim is to consider the impact which the arrival of Roman power had on indigenous British culture, looking particularly at certain settlements and their lifestyles. Evidence for this comes primarily from archaeological sources, so you will need to bear in mind some of the questions and procedures you have just studied; look too for the way literary evidence links in.

You will need to use Goodman, the Offprints Book, the Illustrations Book and the Colour Plates. You will be working fairly independently on this material as this part of the block involves relatively few interactive exercises; instead the sections contain some quite detailed information on which you should be prepared to take notes as and when you wish.

2.1 The Roman conquest of Britain – a historical outline

Exercise

You will be asked in a moment to read a section from Goodman as a general survey of information and issues that will form a background to much of your work on this block. As you will see, this section is the last part of his chapter 21, 'France and Britain', and so a few of his comments pick up on points he has made earlier. Do look back at these if you wish, but as the earlier part of the chapter deals with the Romans in France it is only of background interest here. Certainly Britain had much in common with northern and central parts of France, both in their indigenous culture and in their varied responses to Roman conquest. As northern provinces they also differed from Mediterranean areas, especially the south of France: they had not had a long-term exposure to classical culture, and their societies, climate and physical geography were very different from those of Italy or the Greek East. These shared characteristics obviously provide a wider context in which the British experience can be viewed and are something to keep in mind as you concentrate on Britain.

Goodman
207-16

As you read the Goodman passage, write down the dates (as given on pp.208–11) for Claudius' invasion, Boudicca's revolt, the Roman campaigns in Scotland under Agricola, the building of Hadrian's Wall, and for the building and abandonment of the Antonine Wall. Check the relevant locations against his map (Figure 11) on p.210. (As these dates and places will play a key part in your work in this block, the purpose of this is to equip you with a simple checklist; you do not need to memorize the dates.) You may also find it useful to refer to the Key dates at the end of this block. Please also focus on the questions below as you read through the Goodman passage. They are intended simply to introduce some issues that you meet in greater detail later in the block.

Scotland

1   What does Goodman (p.211) have to say about Roman ambitions about conquering Scotland?

2   How does he describe (p.208) inter-tribal relationships in Britain before the Roman conquest?

3   How does he view (p.212) the British (and French) experience of change brought by the Roman conquest? What kinds of source material does he use (pp.212–16) as evidence about the various reactions to and consequences of Roman rule in Britain?

4   Note down the occasions on which the army is mentioned in Goodman's account.

Please now read through Goodman, pages 207–16, beginning with the section, 'Effects of Roman Conquest'.

Discussion

Later in this block in your work on the northern frontier in Britain you will have a chance to look in greater detail at dates and locations involved in this area, and also at the question of the function and relationship of the two Walls (*was* Hadrian's Wall primarily symbolic?).

1   Note how Goodman's description of the Romans as 'ambivalent' about Scotland (p.211) throws open questions about their reasons for withdrawing from territories which they had conquered there, both in the late first century AD and in the mid second when they abandoned the Antonine Wall. Most important is the question of what the conquest of Scotland meant to successive Roman administrations.

2   The tribal relationships in pre-Roman Britain which Goodman describes (p.208) were complicated by the various origins of the groups. 'Rivalries' (his word) and power struggles between the tribes opened up opportunities for Roman influence. Note how Octavian (Augustus) operated such influence through client kingdoms in the south of England, yet he and Tiberius held back from actual invasion even though this was urged by the client kings for motives of their own. Here Goodman seems to imply that while Romans were prepared to exploit local differences for their own advantage they were not prepared to take the decisive move of invasion without having good reasons of their own.

3   'Drastic' is the word chosen by Goodman (p.212) to describe the changes that followed the Roman invasion of Britain. In fact this repeats what he said when he summed up the impact of Roman rule on local society in Britain and northern Gaul as 'dramatic, sudden and drastic' (p.208).

The force of this word ties in with what has been introduced in the paragraphs immediately preceding this (pp.211–12), which discuss rebellion against Roman rule in the period after the conquest. He graphically illustrates how Roman greed and insensitivity (over taxation and the treatment of local leaders) were factors in this as were other more substantial changes to culture and society. And, according to him, British resentments were sharpened by an awareness that with the Roman invasion 'the last of their culture was under threat' (p.212).

For me this presentation of the scenario in such dramatic, life-or-death terms recalls the image on the sculpture from Aphrodisias (see Plate 4.4), and raises the same questions about the extent to which a polarized view may be justified. We will return to this later, but for the moment note how Goodman goes on to frame a central question about the nature of these cultural changes: he asks about their depth.

Breadth and depth are obviously critical dimensions in any discussions of cultural change: you met them as issues in Essay Four on cultural developments over the empire as a whole. In stressing that 'Variety is to be expected' (p.212) Goodman signals that there is no single answer to this question, as the effects of the changes inevitably varied in depth from one place to another.

So what of Goodman's sources for assessing this type of change in Britain after the conquest? Towns and urban culture are his starting-place. His account of these is useful for the clear contrasts it draws between particular towns (for example, Camulodunum and Verulamium) in function and apparent lifestyle, and in his introduction of the terms *colonia, municipium* and *civitas* (check back in the Glossary if you need to remind yourself of the meanings of these terms, which also occurred in Essay Eight and will be used again later in this block). Note too what Goodman says about the role played by 'local aristocrats' in the towns. You can perhaps make a useful comparison with the situations you studied in the Roman Greek world, particularly in respect of euegertism, the commissioning of public works in towns by wealthy individuals. A second source of evidence is the deployment of local personnel in Roman institutions, such as the Roman senate and the army (as leaders of auxiliary units, which you will be studying later in this block). Here comparison between Britain and northern Gaul is useful in showing how poorly Britain figures in these respects. Goodman explains this in terms of the relatively late date of Britain's conquest which gave Britons a poor chance of securing places of (even) limited power in existing institutions of the Roman empire. So here is one place where it seems that in this early period at least Britain may have got little out of becoming part of the empire. A third source of evidence is to do with religious culture and the treatment of indigenous cults within the new Roman context. Finally, Goodman looks at local economic opportunities which Roman occupation opened up (pp.215–16) and the effect of these on parts of the countryside.

To sum up your answers to this part of the exercise, consider how far Goodman uses the evidence from these sources to argue for assimilation and how far for resistance, particularly to Roman urban culture. How far do you think Goodman really answers his own questions (on p.212) about the extent to which assimilation – and resistance – actually happened? You will be able to test some of your answers to such questions as you work more closely on some of the sources of evidence for yourself. But perhaps the central point to note from this section is that after the experience of conquest, which might have seemed a cultural death-blow to some, Britain did survive the conquest to participate in urban and economic development brought by empire.

4   In the passage you have read there are only limited mentions of the Roman army, which is perhaps surprising given its crucial

role in the conquest of Britain, although its troop movements during the invasion are noted (p.208). But some of the other brief references are worth thinking about as they give insights into various aspects of culture and power in this situation. First are the cultural differences between towns that were *coloniae* (the settlements of Roman army veterans) and others, at least in respect of surviving evidence for the sponsorship of public buildings (p.213). Then there is the matter of employment of local warriors to lead auxiliary units in the army (although it seems questionable whether many Britons were used in this way) (p.214). Finally Goodman mentions how the presence of troops in an area was a stimulus to trade (p.215). These are all pointers to various parts played by the Roman army in Britain's development as well as its conquest. Again, these are factors which you will have a chance to evaluate later.

Naturally, such a brief account of Britain's relation with Rome, both before and during the Roman occupation, glosses over many details and nuances; but it will serve you usefully as an outline of issues, some of which will now be considered further.

2.2   Britain before the Claudian conquest

Even before Caesar's invasions in 55 and 54 BC there were contacts between Rome and Britain through trade, especially via Gaul and Spain, and in the period between these and the final invasion by Claudius in AD 43, Roman influence increased in many ways, in certain parts of the country at least. Yet most of this influence did not come direct from Rome itself, but through contact with the Romanized communities of northern Gaul which had been conquered by the Romans in 50 BC. This is important to remember as it meant that the 'Roman' culture experienced in this way by people in southern Britain was really somewhat mixed. As you will see it seems to have had a particular attraction for the British élites at this time when their societies were making great transitions.

From about 100 BC there seem to have been gradual changes in the lifestyle of south and eastern Britain. These are visible in many aspects of the archaeological record, but are not altogether easy to interpret. It would seem that hill-fort settlements were abandoned, that there was a growth in population and in the number of agricultural settlements, and trade contacts extended. These changes were probably linked to developments in the social structure which can be seen from various sources: there is strong evidence for an emergent élite class which supplied the 'chiefs' or 'kings' known from the series of coins they came

(handwritten margin notes:)

trade contact pre-caesar between Rome + Britain

(Roman influence (silchester for eg) (my note)

Contact from Romanized communities British élites attracted

00BC s/se Britain chges in lifestyle archaeological evidence - not easy to interpret + tho!

Hill-fort settlements abandoned growth in pop. + no. agric. settlements + no. trade contact extended

developments in social structure emergent élite class

26

to mint and from mention by Roman historians. Julius Caesar, for instance, commented that 'The population is numerous, their homesteads clustered together and very like those in Gaul, and there are many cattle. For money they use either bronze or gold coins or iron bars of fixed standard weight' (*The Gallic War* 5.12, my translation). Strabo noted that 'they are ruled by chieftains. The forests are their towns as they fortify a large circular enclosure with trees they have felled, and there they make huts for themselves and their cattle' (4.5.2, my translation). Here is a view of a relatively settled culture, aristocratic in structure and with a developing agriculture and economy.

It is a view largely borne out by the archaeology of Britain in the late Iron Age (that is to say in the hundred years or so before the Claudian invasion: the 'Iron Age' is the conventional archaeological term for the period from about 700 BC until well into the Roman period, characterized by particular social and economic developments). Much of Britain's growing population seems to have been involved in some kind of agriculture and, possibly, limited manufacturing, and the economy was such that it was able to sustain an élite. Warfare must have been the traditional way of securing territories or alliances between the various tribal groups, but probably by the later Iron Age this had largely ceased to be a major social factor although it remained a way of symbolizing power (Millett, 1990, p.35). Gold, used only for personal ornament, was another way in which members of the élite displayed their standing; rich craftsmanship is shown for instance by the great torc (neck-ring) found at Snettisham in Norfolk (Colour Plate 4.1). The bigger settlements cannot be described as towns in the sense that many of them later became under Roman occupation. Known in modern archaeological parlance by the Latin word 'oppida' (singular: 'oppidum'; written without italics they contrast with the terms *oppidum* and *oppida* used to signify small Roman town settlements), they seem to have acted as some focal point for their surrounding society. Some seem to have been quite densely occupied while others were sparser or more diffuse in layout. Many were surrounded by dykes that may have been used as defences or to mark out territory; these dykes and ditches were often linear arrangements (rather than enclosing circles) and sometimes extended over quite large areas.

Finding a meaningful collective name for all the peoples who inhabited Britain at this time is problematic. Goodman, as you saw, adopted a solution that has been common in the past and called them 'Celts', but this is a term which is now very much in question as having been invented by later scholars as a convenient 'umbrella' term to cover non-Roman peoples who were in fact quite diverse. Another solution is to pass over the ethnic aspect and speak instead in terms of the culture of the period: this is what Millett does in the passage which you will be

[Handwritten margin notes: JC; Strabo; settled culture, aristocratic, agric. + economy; Iron Age ? 700 BC into Roman period; growing pop - agriculture - ltd manufacturing - economy to just sustain an élite; warfare no longer major social factor; gold; bigger settlements not towns - 'oppida' - focal point for surrounding society; some densely occupied - some sparsely; dykes + ditches; British not a collective people - not 'celtic' - diverse peoples - rather terms of culture of the period]

reading later from his book on *The Romanization of Britain* where he writes about 'LPRIA', the Later Pre-Roman Iron Age (see also Millett, 1990, p.10). Probably the most useful way to proceed in the context of our discussion is to avoid unnecessary labelling especially in terms of peoples, as this will help to keep questions of culture as open as possible. Certainly it seems to be the case that Britain in the century before the Claudian invasion was a place of cultural development and some diversity.

Major factors in this diversity were the division of the population into various social (or 'tribal') groupings and the fact that the lowland south-east of the country had increasing contact with the Romanized culture of Gaul. Shortly you will be introduced to two settlements in which both these factors play an important part, so it is worth looking at them in slightly more detail.

The evidence used to locate the various tribal groupings in late Iron Age Britain (as in Goodman, p.209, Figure 10) comes from various sources. Some tribes were mentioned by Roman writers (although of course their source of evidence was not always reliable): Julius Caesar, for instance, separates indigenous Britons in the interior from 'Belgic immigrants' on the coast who still bore the names of their original tribes (*The Gallic War* V 12). The groupings which Romans used as a basis for the *civitates* which they set up after the conquest (and which you will be meeting shortly) also provides some retrospective indications. But perhaps some of the most interesting information comes from the emergent British coinage. Coins can give the names of some historical personages and show something of the changing interactions between different tribes across different territories. The case of the Catuvellauni is a good illustration of this. The tribe seems to have expanded from its earlier location around modern Hertfordshire and eventually linked (somehow) in the early first century AD with the Trinovantes in Essex. Together they formed a powerful grouping. Coins of their leader Cunobelinus or Cunobelin (Shakespeare's Cymbeline) were issued from Colchester, then from Verulamium (St Albans) and have been found later in Kent and in northern Hampshire. Quite possibly it was this kind of expansionism that caused the internal conflicts which apparently led some British leaders to seek refuge with Augustus as suppliants (as he himself commemorates in his *Res Gestae* 32. Later on Cunobelin in his turn seems to have expelled one of his sons, Adminius, who sought protection with the Roman emperor Gaius (Caligula) (Suetonius, *Gaius* 44). All in all, these various sources combine to give a working knowledge of the general location of these groupings in the pre-Roman period, and in certain cases some useful information about historical changes in territory and rulers.

Another major ingredient in the development of late Iron Age Britain was the varying degree of contact with the Romanized lifestyle that operated across the Channel, particularly in the period after Caesar's invasions. In terms of trade patterns with the Continent, it is possible to map out three different sectors of Britain (see Plate 4.6 in the Illustrations Book): a core zone in the south-east that was in direct contact with Roman culture; a peripheral swathe surrounding this which seems to have supplied goods to the core in exchange for Roman products or coins; and an outer zone exploited perhaps for slaves. The Roman geographer Strabo, writing at the time of Augustus, described (iv, 5, 3) some of the luxury goods that passed between Britain and Gaul – ivory, amber, glass and jewellery and the income which Rome made in taxing these. In the south-east of England, Roman luxury goods found in Iron Age burials reflect these trading patterns or gift exchange. Plate 4.7 shows a reconstruction of one such burial found at Welwyn, Hertfordshire; it included many items imported from Gaul and further afield in the Roman world. Among them were the small silver cups shown in Plate 4.8.

But these two factors which I have just sketched out – the socio-political developments and the cultural contacts – do not necessarily fit together. It was certainly the case that in the north and west of Britain both factors operated rather differently from in the south, probably stimulated by the further factor of the physical geography which inhibited large settlements or the development of a prosperous agriculture. While there were some powerful tribal groups in the north, there were not the wealthy élites ready to pick up on the attractions of a Roman lifestyle that there were in the south-east. Yet even in the south-east of the country there was ambivalence about Roman influence. As it has been observed: 'The leaders of the Catuvellauni kingdom never showed any disinclination to import either amphorae, whether of wine or other delicacies, or other luxury items of Roman origin, however far they were moving politically in a direction likely to incur Roman hostility' (Salway, 1997, p.49). In other words, Roman power and Roman culture could elicit rather different responses, especially when the Britons in question had become as powerful a force in the area as the Catuvellauni.

Two important centres for the Catuvellauni were Verlamion and Camulodunon, which in Roman times came to be known by their Latinized names of Verulamium and Camulodunum (and are now St Albans and Colchester: see Goodman, p.210, Figure 11 for their position in Britain). I want to follow them through from their pre-Roman states (in this section) to the developments which occurred as a consequence of the Roman conquest when they had contrasting experiences (in the next section of the block).

locus (handwritten)

Verulamium (handwritten)

Figure 4.2 *Silver coin of Tasciovanus, marked* VER, *minted at Verlamion in the first half of the first century* AD, *British Museum, London. (© The British Museum)*

The importance of Verlamion for the Catuvellauni is reflected in coins minted there by Tasciovanus *c.* 15 BC to AD 10, some of which carry the abbreviation 'VER' (Figure 4.2). The settlement seems to have originated at Prae Wood and expanded from there down towards the river Ver, resulting perhaps in a number of different subsidiary centres which covered a large site enclosed within a system of ditches. Plate 4.9 shows clearly that it was a sprawling settlement, including areas beyond the later site of the Roman town, enclosed defences marked as a dotted line. One of these outlying areas may have been a religious centre, and the settlement at Gorhambury was agricultural. The large number of coin moulds discovered, particularly towards the river, indicates some extensive metal-working activities. There is evidence in the cemetery sites of some high-status burials dating from AD 1–60 (that is to say into the period after the Roman arrival) which show the influence of Romanized Gaul not only in grave-goods imported as luxuries from various parts of the Roman world, but in their use of cremation as a method of disposing of the body. In fact one cemetery, south-west of the site of the Roman town, has been found to contain over 450 burials, within seven ditched enclosures, which each contained a rich central burial surrounded by many others.

Similar elements can be seen in the archaeology of Camulodunon where settlements and burials as well as the evidence of local coinage attest its significance as a local centre. Initially it seems to have belonged to the Trinovantes but certainly by AD 5, Cunobelin, of the Catuvallauni, was issuing coins from there (see Colour Plate 4.2, which shows a gold coin of Cunobelin). By 25 BC Camulodunon seems to have consisted of various small settlements protected by a series of extensive dykes and earthworks, with concentrations at the two sites of Sheepen and Gosbecks. Plate 4.10 shows these dykes in relation to the later sites of the Roman *colonia* (which you will meet later in the block) and of the modern town of Colchester: notice how widespread the Iron Age features are, and that they lie at some distance from the later *colonia*.

There is archaeological evidence to show that agricultural activities at Gosbecks were centred on an important farm and religious sanctuary, and that there was some industry at Sheepen. Amongst the evidence of metal-working there have been found moulds for coins issued by

Camulodunon (handwritten)

Cunobelin. It has been suggested that he lived in the farmstead at Gosbecks which was surrounded by its own enclosures, and that Gosbecks became a centre for local assembly.

But perhaps the most spectacular evidence for the culture of local rulers comes from a series of burial sites in the area, thought to be associated with them and their families. The Lexden Tumulus, dated to the late first century BC, may have housed the remains of king Addedomaros (its site lies slightly to the south-east of the number 4 on Plate 4.10). Along with the cremation were buried a wide range of goods almost all ritually broken, many of them luxury imports. These include cast metal ornaments, chain mail, some fragments of a gold tissue fabric, objects decorated with red glass, amphorae, and most significant of all for our purposes, a silver medallion made out of a coin of Augustus dated 18–16 BC (shown in Plate 4.11). The fact that this was placed as a treasured possession in the tumulus suggests strong positive feelings towards things Roman, if not actual contacts with Rome at this time. At Stanway, the burial site (Plate 4.10, number 8) seems to have operated over a period of time from the late first century BC to about AD 60 (that is to say, as at Verlamion, into the period of Roman settlement and up to the Boudiccan revolt). Essentially it comprises four large burial chambers, each set in an enclosure (which also include some secondary burials); they may have been used as a place for high-class funerals prior to cremation, and here, too, grave goods seem to have been ritually destroyed. Finally, the layout of the enclosure at Gosbecks (Plate 4.10, number 7) where the temple was later built in the Roman period, has suggested that it might have housed the burial place of Cunobelin himself. But even though this remains uncertain, the rest of the evidence from Camulodunon throws some vivid light on the culture of the community in the fifty or so years before the Roman invasion, and especially on that of their rulers: their aristocratic warrior background is clear, as are the indications of their contacts with the Roman world.

To sum up this section, I think it is possible to say that there is now a good deal of important source material available for studying Britain in the period before the Roman conquest. In places such as Verlamion and Camulodunon, we can see the range of activities that they supported and how these relate to the rather extended nature of the settlements; we have indications of their social structures and cultural values, and – most important for the argument of this part of the block – we have an increasingly good picture of just how much these were influenced through contacts with Roman culture (in some form or another) in the century or so before the Claudian conquest. Quite probably further significant discoveries will be made before this course has finished.

But a crucial ingredient of any study of Britain at this time are the questions asked and the standpoints taken. Of course these are always

[Handwritten margin notes: N13 / reassess culture of Pre-Roman Britain + impact of their arrival. Did Romans bring 'progress' + improvement or just 'something different'?]

important in reconstructing the past, but arguably they are even more so in a case like this where views of pre-Roman (and indeed 'Roman') Britain have been so heavily coloured by the value that scholars traditionally placed on classical Roman culture and on the writings of Roman historians. This has often led to the judgement that the advent of Roman culture brought definite 'progress' to Iron Age Britain. Here perhaps, in a post-colonial context and one where archaeological material is more valued and better understood than once it was, there are opportunities to reassess the culture that existed in Britain before the Romans came, as well as the impact of their actual arrival. Did the Romans necessarily bring 'progress' and 'improvement', or simply something different? These are big questions which cannot be answered in the restricted space of the following sections, but they are crucial to have in mind as they shape our various interpretations of this period of history. Some of these questions will recur in the last part of this block, which is on 'Presenting Roman Britain'; they also throw up the whole issue of how far such value judgements are appropriate or useful in our consideration of the past (and you will come back to this issue again in Block Five).

2.3   Britain in the post-conquest years: *civitas, colonia* and client kingdoms

Claudius' invasion of Britain in AD 43 had an inevitable and major impact on the country. It made a decisive change in Britain's relationship with Rome and forced the leaders of the British tribes into new political situations as the Romans sought to consolidate their power. This they did in various ways which have a close bearing on the interactions of culture, identity and power.

Tacitus gives a pithy account of how the Romans went about this, having secured the victory.

> The first of the men of consular rank appointed as governor was Aulus Plautius, and after him Ostorius Scapula, both excellent at war. Little by little the part nearest [to the Continent] was reduced into the usual form of a province and a colony of military veterans was added. Certain of the tribes [*civitates*] were given to Cogidumnus as king. This was in accordance with the long accepted Roman habit of making even kings instruments for the imposition of servitude.
>
> (Tacitus, *Agricola* 14, trans. Salway)

In this section I want to look at three arrangements which featured in Tacitus' description – *civitas, colonia* and client kingdoms – to consider the parts they played in the Roman strategy for 'reducing' Britain into 'the usual form of a province' once areas were released from initial military control. To do so I shall concentrate on the two places we have just considered, known under the Romans as Verulamium and Camulodunum. As Goodman noted in his chapter on Britain (more specifically his pp.212–13), they present contrasting profiles of development under the Romans. Verulamium was made a local administrative centre as a *civitas* capital while Camulodunum became a *colonia* for the settlement of Roman veteran soldiers. But in AD 60–61 they both came to share the same fate, being destroyed in the Boudiccan revolt against Roman rule. After that each was rebuilt and enjoyed further developments, but it is the period up to their destruction that is being considered here.

In each case the key question you should ask yourself as you work on the material is how far the arrival of the Romans seems to have changed matters. Power structures (as mediated, for instance, through the legal status of the settlement and through the élites who ran it), new buildings and urban development, and the response of local inhabitants are important topics in which to search for some answers.

Civitas capital and *municipium*

As their military thrust moved towards the north and west, the Roman authorities created self-governing units in parts of the south and east, following a strategy which they had employed in Gaul. These were termed *civitates* (singular: *civitas*) and had their own administrative capitals which were often sited in or close to locations where there had been tribal centres and/or Roman army installations. Romans laid out these small towns and invested them with appropriate facilities and buildings, but they left in place the local laws and social structures and did not grant Roman citizenship to the inhabitants who were left with the status of *peregrini* (foreigners). The underlying aim of these moves was to create stable and flourishing local societies managed by their own élites, who would in turn be motivated to support Roman culture by what they had gained from it personally. So whereas the Romans actually held overall power in the country, the continued role of local élites in running the *civitates* and their capitals was intended to suggest to the local population that life continued much as it had done before the Romans came.

The first to be created in England were the *civitas* of the Cantiaci with its capital at Canterbury and a *civitas* which probably included the southern groups of the Catuvellauni tribe with its centre at Verulamium. (Possibly there was another for the Trinovantes but this is uncertain because the *colonia* at Colchester was sited in their territory.)

Verulamium impt
settlemt pre-Roman.
under roman army
small fort-site,
Watling st ran
thro' it.

claudius -
gnd plan,
defensive wall +
ditch

evidence of
Metal-working
workshops

Tacitus descubes
verulamium as a
Municipium -
not known when
actually was
tho'.

As we have already seen, in its pre-Roman days the settlement at Verulamium was a place of some importance. Under its brief occupation by the Roman army it seems to have been the site of a small fort, and Watling Street, the Roman road which linked London and the Midlands, ran through it. These factors probably stimulated its early development as a *civitas* capital, and during the reign of Claudius the small town was laid out on a simple grid plan and was given a defensive wall and ditch (see Plate 4.12). Of the buildings whose traces have been uncovered perhaps the most significant is a block of timber construction, fronting on to Watling Street. Its apparent use as metal-working workshops at some stage suggests that by AD 50 Verulamium was modestly involved in manufacture and trade. Nothing more is known of the town until it is mentioned in accounts of its sacking by Boudicca. Perhaps it was a target for British attack because of its Romanized culture: in his account of its destruction, Tacitus describes it as a *municipium* (*Annals* 14.33; you will read this passage from Tacitus later, as extract 4.3). This was a town which enjoyed higher status than a *civitas* capital, and was often a title bestowed on existing provincial communities. It gave certain of the rights of Roman citizenship to the community as a whole, and effectively full citizenship to those who had held certain official positions. It was an important element in the gradual integration of the provincial peoples into the Roman state. But whether in fact Verulamium had actually acquired this status – and if so it would have been rather speedy – or whether Tacitus, who was writing some thirty years later, had got it wrong, is unclear. However, the description does at least point to the status (and prosperity) which Verulamium came to enjoy when rebuilt after its destruction by Boudicca.

how far did roman
conquest after
lifestyle > town?

pre-Roman
settlemt
flourishing

Roman -
rectilinear plan -
buildings -
timber buildings

The question to consider here is just how far the Roman conquest actually altered the lifestyle of the town. Any answer is likely to come from archaeological evidence. As we have seen there is plenty such evidence to suggest that the pre-Roman settlement was a flourishing place of some standing: it produced coinage, practised agriculture and metal-working. What more did the creation of the Roman *civitas* bring? One obvious feature was the new rectilinear town plan. Another feature was its buildings, and in particular the timber building already mentioned, which has been seen as contributing particularly significant evidence for this question: its function, design and mode of construction have been cited and used in the debate about the impact of Rome on Verulamium – and thence in the much wider debate about Roman policies of urban development. To see how evidence from such details can play a major part in so potentially wide an argument, it is worth looking now at how it has been used.

Exercise

Offprint 4.2 (from Millett, 1990, pp.62–72) gives an account of this usage of archaeological evidence. (This excerpt is the first part of Millett's discussion of the development of towns in the *civitates*.) The main question to bear in mind when you read it is: what does Millett's argument imply about the 'skills, resources and motivation' of the local population independent of any Roman intervention?

Please read offprint 4.2 now.

Discussion

The implication is, I think, quite straightforward: that evidence of the timber building does not inevitably indicate that the Roman army was the only possible source of the necessary expertise. This conclusion in turn must challenge a view of the Roman contribution to urban development in early Britain that relates too closely to Tacitus' account in *Agricola* 21 (and from your work on the audio cassette interview with David Braund you may remember this passage as a much-quoted excerpt). Comparative evidence suggests that constructions of this type were around in Britain before the Romans came, so the building in Verulamium (despite its classical-looking porticos) may be attributable to local resources and motivation.

That said, I think that we need to be careful here to avoid jumping to conclusions. A close reading of the evidence Millett adduces in support of his argument about architectural styles in the British Later Pre-Roman Iron Age (LPRIA) shows that the rectangular designs are 'perhaps Romanized', while some of the comparative material is in fact uncertain in terms of technological details or dating. However, the central point of his argument stands; that is, to warn against an immediate assumption that only Roman craftsmen would have had the know-how to build in this way. This caveat then makes it possible to acknowledge that the post-conquest development of Verulamium was not necessarily as dependent on decisive Roman intervention as had been argued before; instead this one major piece of evidence can be part of an argument for a greater continuity of local cultural traditions.

There is also evidence that the Romanization of the town did not exclude the continuation of local traditions at least amongst the local élite. The remains have been found at Folly Lane (in present-day St Albans) of an imposing cremation burial probably of a local chief who must have died around AD 55. The grave goods burned in it include

35

grave goods incl.
Roman-style
luxury items -
indicates co-existence
of Roman + Brit.
cultures.

many Roman-style luxury items (silver vessels, amphorae, and a Roman-style couch, for instance) as well as a coat of iron mail armour of the type worn by Celtic auxiliaries. Perhaps this was a highly exceptional situation in honour of a British leader of high standing; even so, it is evidence for the co-existence of Roman and British cultures, reflected in burial practice and in the array of material goods.

Colonia

Colchester

At Colchester something very different happened: 'the symbolic heart of Cunobelinus' former kingdom was immediately obliterated by a Roman fort that incorporated earthworks that had formed the entrance to the royal compound and the tribal sacred enclosure' (Salway, 1997, p.70).

Romans set up
own settlement with
rtd soldiers-
probly confiscated
land

settlent had
power over locals
symbol. Roman
rule in Britain

In other words, the Roman authorities there chose to work on an opposite principle to that which lay behind the development of the *civitas*. Rather than working through existing local social structures, they set up a settlement of their own with retired soldiers, probably confiscating land to do so. This settlement not only had actual power over the locals but was a symbol of Roman rule in Britain. It gave a clear message of 'them' and 'us'.

Trinovantes +
Catuvellauni [ppwy -
Colchester site signif.
became
Claudius' prime
objective.
2 units Roman army
stationed there -
cavalry, small fort
gosbecks
legion lger fort built
c.AD44 (town centre
now) lge fort redundant
when legion to wales -
Roman veteran
soldiers took over as
retirement site...
strong Roman presence
kept in area

The historical background to this is the powerful position of the Trinovantes and Catuvellauni at the time of the conquest and the significance of the site at Colchester in this context. It is not surprising, therefore, that Claudius made it his prime objective, and having taken the site, set about overstamping it with symbols of Roman control. In the years immediately after the conquest, two units of the Roman army, the Twentieth Legion and an auxiliary unit of Thracian cavalry, were kept stationed there. The cavalry unit may have occupied a small fort built by the Romans by the British site at Gosbecks, while the legion had a larger fort built in about AD 44 in what is now the town centre (Plate 4.10 shows these two different locations: Gosbecks is number 7, and the legionary fort is marked as the '*colonia*'). This fort became redundant when the legion was sent off to fight in Wales and it was turned over to accommodation for Roman veteran soldiers. As retirement homes these barracks may have been initially rather unattractive but as an established *colonia* they were an effective way of retaining a strong Roman presence in the area.

1st Colonia in Britain

coloniae in other
parts of empire -
dispossession of
locals probable

Although this *colonia* at Camulodunum was the first in Britain (which was to have others at Gloucester, Lincoln and, much later, at York), it had many precedents in the Roman world. You read in Block Two (and in Essay Eight) about Augustus' settlement of veterans and the establishment of *coloniae* at places such as Aosta, which gave the wider context in terms of Roman imperial practice. It involved setting up a town with its own administration and set of laws, and making a grant of land in the surrounding territory on which the veterans could farm; as at Colchester this might mean that locals were dispossessed.

The archaeological evidence shows how the site at Colchester was taken over almost intact from the legionary fort. Compare the layout of the two in the simple plans of the fort (top) and the *colonia* (bottom) in Plate 4.13. Some military buildings survived in use as they were (at least up to the time when the whole site was destroyed in Boudicca's rebellion), but some barracks and centurions' quarters in Culver Street and Lion Walk were converted into houses. Parts of the old military defences were levelled to provide more space for the large public buildings. There are archaeological remains of the great temple of Claudius, a theatre and an arch, while Tacitus also refers to a council chamber and a statue of Victory. Careful archaeological dating of individual buildings suggests that all this conversion work took several years and that the eastern part of the colony in the former annexe of the fort was not laid out until the mid 50s AD. It has been argued that the temple with its dedication to the divine Claudius could not have been built until after the emperor's death in AD 54 (because divine status would have been inappropriate during his lifetime). The name of the colony at this stage is unknown, although when it was rebuilt after the Boudiccan revolt it was known as the *Colonia Victricensis* ('The Colony of Victory').

The resulting town must have been imposing, and in its very name and layout a reminder of the Roman military background. The temple of Claudius (Plate 4.14) would have reinforced the message: it was the centre of the imperial cult in Britain, huge and classical in design. The bronze portrait head of Claudius (Plate 4.15) may have belonged to an equestrian statue that was a prominent part of its display.

So here in the *colonia* a small Rome was re-created, with Roman citizens, its own set of Roman laws and administrative structures, Roman buildings and leisure pursuits, and in the imperial cult the presence of the emperor himself. Preserved in the layer of burned debris that resulted from the destruction of the town by Boudicca in AD 60 were dates and figs imported from the Mediterranean.

Exercise

To conclude this section you may find it helpful to list what you see as the possible benefits and disadvantages which the establishment of the *colonia* brought to the Romans and to the Britons.

Discussion

To the Romans the most obvious benefit must have been the chance of stability that the settlement appeared to promise. Certainly,

Tacitus reports its purpose in those terms: 'a colony with a strong group of veteran soldiers was established on conquered land at Camulodunum, as a protection against revolt and to imbue the locals with a respect for law and government' (*Annals* 12.32, my translation). Such colonies increased the chance of a peaceful settlement of the area for the Romans: they introduced a loyal band of Roman citizens who initially, at least, could show military expertise if needed. Furthermore, by settling veterans in sites of former legionary fortresses in provinces such as Britain, Roman authorities avoided greater problems of finding land for them in Italy.

But what of the locals? It is not hard to imagine that they might have had mixed feelings. After all, colonies such as these were artificial units, often imposed by Roman invaders on to the pattern of native settlements which had grown up more organically over time. This was no exception. On the one hand it may have encouraged trade and prosperity around the Roman masters. On the other, the confiscation of land from local inhabitants for the benefit of Roman veterans, who unlike the locals were citizens of Rome, had the potential to upset existing local patterns of power and wealth.

Yet at Colchester there is some interesting and important archaeological evidence to suggest that the establishment of the colony did not disrupt some of the existing customs and practices of the local British community. The Roman authorities seem to have acted with some sensitivity towards the Gosbecks site and later allowed developments of the local sanctuary there, while élite British burials seem to have continued at Stanway after the establishment of the *colonia* up to the time of the revolt against the Romans in AD 60. Some of the grave goods from the site suggest a fairly cultured lifestyle: for instance, a surgical kit and an inkpot were found in secondary burials.

To find in the archaeological record evidence for British discontent at the loss of land and status and resentment of the high-handed treatment meted out by the Romans, we need to look primarily at the results of the uprising in AD 60, although slave chains and shattered human bones (whether Roman or Briton) found in earlier contexts suggest that the situation had been troubled before then. The archaeological evidence shows that the rebels' attack was ferocious and this seems to support the view given by Tacitus (*Annals* 14.31) that British resentment at the loss of land was one of the major motivating factors in the revolt.

Client kings

With 'client kings' we turn to a rather different scenario which did not involve Romans in direct settlement or overt domination of these areas of Britain. The questions about culture, identity and power raised by this arrangement are therefore somewhat different from those we have been considering so far: theoretically at least it allowed the local communities to retain, for the most part, their own traditional expressions of all three.

In the passage of *Agricola* 14 quoted at the start of section 2.3, Tacitus described the use of client kings as a 'long-accepted' practice in Roman strategies of government. It certainly played an important part in the early decades of empire (as you had reason to note in Block Two; see also Goodman, pp.110–12) although by the time of Nero, direct rule came to be preferred. In Britain after the invasion the client kingdoms were another way by which Romans promoted their influence through local leaders. By formalizing agreements with rulers of lands which abutted on their territories, Romans could keep some control over local events whilst at the same time allowing the client states an apparent independence in return for their support. There were three client kingdoms in Britain, with rather different backgrounds and eventual fates. Plate 4.16 shows how this division appears to have worked in geographical terms. On the south coast, Cogidubnus (also known as Cogidumnus) was awarded the territory that had probably belonged to the Atrebates under their king Verica who had allegedly been one of the British leaders who had urged the Romans to invade. Although Cogidubnus remains a shadowy figure in the sources, it looks as if his client kingdom worked successfully. From the Roman standpoint this might be a case of 'no news being good news' since both the other kingdoms turned out to threaten the security of the whole Roman enterprise in Britain, and in suppressing these difficulties, the Romans ended this arrangement of co-existence with supposedly friendly client rulers, and took all the territories into their control. In the north were the Brigantes about whom relatively little is known. They appear to have been a group of different tribes rather than a single one but were headed by a powerful queen, Cartimandua. In the end, in about AD 69, internal factions in the kingdom led to a final Roman intervention.

But it is the third client kingdom I want to concentrate on here, not least because the events which saw its end were those which precipitated the destruction of the other two places we have looked at, Verulamium and Camulodunum, through the rebellion of Boudicca. This was the kingdom of the Iceni, ruled by Prasutagus, which occupied territory in present-day Norfolk.

Having allied themselves with Rome at the invasion, the Iceni were left after it as an independent state without a Roman presence and were apparently allowed to retain their weapons. Perhaps they had expected that matters would continue like this, because unlike most of their neighbouring tribes they had kept their culture relatively free from contact with Rome in the years preceding invasion, even to the point of excluding Roman traders. But relations with Rome began to deteriorate. In AD 47, Publius Ostorius Scapula, the Roman provincial governor, included communities of the Iceni in his measures to increase Roman control of the area and they were required to disarm. This was the point of the first small-scale revolt, which resulted in defeat of the rebellious Iceni and a fort being built in their territory. Then in AD 60, the Icenian king Prasutagus died. It seems that Roman officials rushed in plundering the territory and abusing his widow, Boudicca, and their daughters as if the kingdom had been conquered. What was more, leading Romans (including Seneca) who had put money into Britain called in their loans. These actions were the final straw for the Britons. In their move to retaliate, the Iceni found willing allies in disaffected members of the neighbouring Trinovantes who had lost land and money through the establishment of the *colonia* of Camulodunum in their territory, and had been suffering harsh punishment at Roman hands. A major revolt, led by Boudicca, began.

Much of this is described by Tacitus and Cassius Dio in accounts which you will be reading in the last part of the block (extracts 4.3, 4.4 and 4.5), and supporting evidence exists in the archaeological record. Hoards found near Iceni settlements of this time include Roman as well as Icenian coins, which may reflect an influx of Roman money into the area before the revolt, partly perhaps as loan. But perhaps the most vivid evidence is for the sheer extent of the destruction carried out by the Britons on the Roman *colonia*, which in itself testifies to the ferocity of feeling against the place and all that it stood for. (You will be seeing some of this evidence, in the form of material displayed in the Castle museum at Colchester, in the last video sequence of the block.) The inhabitants of the colony (many of whom had gathered for protection in the temple of Claudius) were killed, and the town was burned down. The burnt debris survives as a distinct layer in the archaeological record of the site and though it has the positive value for modern archaeologists of providing a clear means of dating material, for Romans at the time it was a totally negative and humiliating experience. Not only did the Iceni attack with fire but they seem to have destroyed or looted Roman statues, including, quite possibly, the bronze image of Claudius (Plate 4.15), from which this head was so obviously broken off, and they overturned and damaged tombstones of Roman soldiers in the cemeteries (Plates 4.17 and 4.18).

To sum up the ground covered in this part of the block, the central issue has been a comparison of Britain before and after Claudius' invasion. Given the brief space we have had here in which to look at this rather complex picture – and this is definitely a case where the picture is dependent on close reading of a good deal of small-scale evidence – this has inevitably been rather a limited survey. However, you have looked in some detail at changes that seem to have occurred in the culture and power structures in some specific areas in south-east Britain. You saw how the Roman authorities seem to have used various approaches to managing the communities they encountered in their newly-conquered territory, working towards shaping it (as Tacitus wrote in the passage of *Agricola* 14 quoted at the start of section 2.3) 'into the usual form of a province'. You also saw how these different approaches affected the existing local societies in different ways – through the reshaping of their towns, for instance, and the erection of new 'Roman' buildings, through the legal status of the various settlements and their inhabitants, and through local experience of Roman power. What was this experience? In describing the British revolt of AD 60–61, Tacitus is outspoken about Roman abuse of power and neglect of responsibility in Britain, and even though it is clear that these expressions are part of his bigger agenda about the workings of central power in Rome (as you heard David Braund discuss earlier), they evoke a sense that the Britons in this area had somehow reached the end of their tether. Goodman in fact suggests that 'the desperate viciousness of much of the fighting may be seen as a mark of the natives' awareness that the last of their culture was under threat' (p.212). But was this the overall reaction of the Britons? It is not so easy to tell, nor is it realistic to generalize, given the range of people and communities involved. Roman power and culture would have impacted differently in different places. If the literary accounts are to be believed, the British rebels seem to have attacked the inhabitants of Romanized towns (London and Verulamium) indiscriminately, doubtless killing many fellow Britons as well as Roman incomers, and this might suggest a power struggle that did not limit itself to Romans and their institutions. The revolt was a turning-point in many senses for social and cultural developments in Roman Britain, and you will be returning to it in the last part of the block, on presenting Romans and Britons.

It is time now to look more closely at an important element of the Roman presence in Britain, namely the army. What was its function? What of its serving soldiers and their cultural identity? In what sense were they Romans? And how did the culture brought by the Roman army impact on the life of frontier zones in northern Britain, different in place and time from *civitas, colonia* and client kingdom in south-east England?

Tacitus
N13

Part Three: The army and Roman Britain

BY VALERIE HOPE AND JANET HUSKINSON

Introduction

In this part of the block you will consider an important group within the population of Roman Britain – the soldiers of the Roman army. You will need *Experiencing Rome*, the Illustrations Book, the Supplementary Texts, Goodman, Lewis and Reinhold, the Colour Plates and video cassette 2.

The exploration of the military presence within any province of the Roman empire raises issues relating to culture, identity and power. In Block One you considered the importance of the army to the emperor; the military machine was the basis of the emperor's power. Here you will explore this issue further by assessing why the emperor maintained such a vast fighting force. Block One also investigated how military prowess played an integral part in the process of emperor evaluation. A good emperor needed to present himself as a soldier and military commander to engender the required loyalty among both soldiers and civilians. Claudius gained a military reputation from the invasion of Britain during the early years of his reign. But he spent only a few days on the island and in general Claudius and his successors were far removed from the provinces and their troops. How was the loyalty of the soldiers maintained? Certain elements such as good pay, loyalty to standards and the swearing of oaths were mentioned in Block One, Part Two, section 2.2 and you may find it useful to reread this section before proceeding further. Here in Part Three, you will explore how the soldier's commitment to the military could act as a vehicle for loyalty to the emperor and also the degree to which the army functioned as a society within a society. This will raise important issues concerning both military culture and the identity of individual soldiers. How did the soldiers, recruited from across the empire and serving in places distant from Rome, perceive themselves, and how were they perceived by others?

3.1 Serving emperor and empire

Without the Roman army there would have been no empire. Yet the Roman army was in its origins a temporary and *ad hoc* organization. Troops were recruited from the citizens of Rome when they were needed and disbanded when they were not. It was not until Augustus that army service became formalized and regulated. The transition from republic to empire had revealed that leading politicians could exploit the military. By contrast, autocratic government, by its very definition, placed the army under the command of one man rather than many men. The imperial army was the tool of the emperor and he had to face the responsibility of organizing and controlling the troops.

In this section you will consider both the role of the army and that of individual soldiers. Why did men join the army and what could they expect from it? For your work in this section you will require Goodman, Lewis and Reinhold and the Supplementary Texts.

Controlling the empire

Exercise

Please now read Goodman, pages 81–6, and make notes on the following question.

In Goodman's opinion, what was the emperor's army for?

To help answer this question you may find it useful to make notes under the following headings:

1 the different types of army units and where they were stationed;

2 the possible reasons why so many troops were needed.

Discussion

1 The type of unit most often referred to in Goodman's discussion is the legion. For example, Goodman notes that in 30 BC there were sixty legions under Octavian's control. The legion was the traditional fighting unit of the Roman army recruited from Roman citizens. In addition there were auxiliary units of cavalry and light infantry and also a navy. Goodman states that the navy, like the auxiliary units, was manned by non-citizen provincials (Goodman, p.84). Indeed the main distinction between legionary and auxiliary troops appears to have been one of legal status rather than fundamental differences in skills and training. In terms of overall numbers, the auxiliary forces probably equalled the legions. The legionaries and auxiliaries were distributed throughout the empire. At the death of Augustus in AD 14 there were twenty-five legions mainly located in the frontier provinces. No legionary or auxiliary troops were located in Rome or Italy. Augustus and his successors, however, were not unprotected in the capital. The Praetorian and Urban cohorts were present for policing duties

and the emperor's protection, while the early emperors also employed specialized troops as a bodyguard.

2   Augustus maintained a large standing army. After victory and the establishment of peace, Augustus did not dismiss all the troops but maintained twenty-eight legions and a substantial number of auxiliary units. Goodman suggests that over 250,000 men were on the army payrolls. This was both a huge expense and a responsibility for emperor and empire. Goodman notes three possible reasons why it was felt necessary to maintain such a vast fighting force:

(a)   Augustus needed to keep campaigning, to keep winning victories and expanding the empire since a military reputation helped to justify his position.

(b)   The troops were needed to protect the existing empire and to guard the frontiers from outside attack.

(c)   Large numbers of men under arms were needed to suppress internal rather than external threats. Military autocracy sought to destroy dissent.

Goodman is sceptical about the first two reasons. Expansion and defence were elements in the imperial policy of many emperors but in themselves did not demand such huge numbers of soldiers. Goodman notes how campaigns often employed a limited number of men; the campaigns of Augustus, for example, never required more than ten legions at any one time. Goodman also suggests that the frontiers could have been protected and defended by a much smaller army. For Goodman the scale of the army reflected its overall role – to protect the emperor and ensure his position. The vast number of troops guaranteed an environment of 'state terror' even if this was not openly acknowledged. Few would dare to challenge the authority of the all-powerful emperor.

For Goodman, then, the Roman army had less to do with the protection of the empire and everything to do with the protection of the emperor. You should remember, however, that the welfare of the empire was entwined with the welfare of the emperor, and thus it is often not easy to distinguish between the relative dangers of external versus internal threats and the appropriate deployment of troops. Equally the priorities of all periods and emperors may not have been the same. Some emperors actively sought a military reputation while others did not. Some emperors faced genuine threats to the frontiers while others did not.

[handwritten margin notes:] NB Goodman's belief army to protect emp! + ensure his pos! 'state terror'

[handwritten margin note:] did emps. had dbl agendas

Being a Roman soldier

One upshot of the military autocracy was, in Goodman's opinion, a general surfeit of soldiers. You may wish to question whether the Roman army was actually too big. Considering the size of the empire, was a force of 250,000 men out of proportion? Nevertheless Goodman suggests that the empire was filled with troops with little soldiering to do. At page 82 Goodman says: 'For most of Augustus' rule, two-thirds of the legions were idle' and later on the same page he says of the soldiers, 'Most of them had nothing to do'. Again, at page 84 Goodman says that troops in Egypt 'had almost nothing to do'.

How fair are these statements? What did a soldier do? The ability to answer such questions is limited by the nature of the available evidence. Literature provides few insights; historians, biographers and poets might record great victories and important campaigns but were little interested

Figure 4.3 *Fragmentary writing tablet from Vindolanda, from Bowman and Thomas, 1983, plate 1.1 (By permission of Dr A Bowman and the Society for the Promotion of Roman Studies) (See extract 4.2 for a translation of the text)*

[handwritten margin notes: Surfeit of soldiers? 250,000 – little soldiering. True?]

45

in the soldier's daily routine. A few exceptional literary works do focus on the army but these often idealize the greatness of the Roman military machine and describe fighting skills and tactics (as in the passage from Vegetius which you will read in a few moments). The most significant records of military activity in peace time come from inscriptions and military documents. Inscriptions often record individual soldiers and military units employed in building activities, worshipping the gods or commemorating the dead. More unusual, but no less fascinating, are dossiers of military records such as papyri from Egypt and the writing tablets discovered at Vindolanda in Britain (see Figure 4.3) which record the day-to-day running of the army and the types of work in which the troops were employed.

Exercise

Please read the following passages. What types of activities were the soldiers regularly engaged in?

Vegetius, 'Military training' in Lewis and Reinhold, pages 451–3;

'Hadrian reviews the garrison of Africa' in Lewis and Reinhold, pages 460–62;

Papyrus texts, 'Movements and transfers of troops', in Lewis and Reinhold, pages 462–4;

Supplementary Texts, extract 4.2, Vindolanda writing tablets (one of which is illustrated in Figure 4.3).

Discussion

Vegetius, who wrote a manual on military matters during the late empire, lists the types of skills in which soldiers were expected to be trained: the soldier should be able to march, leap, swim and carry heavy packs. Vegetius also indicates the occurrence of regular drills and exercises such as practice marches and daily weapons training.

The record of the speech made by the emperor Hadrian in North Africa in AD 128 also highlights the importance of careful and regular training. Hadrian praises different units for their skills and for the adeptness they have demonstrated in order to impress him. In particular he mentions javelin-throwing, construction of entrenchments, wall-building and cavalry exercises. Hadrian begins his speech, however, by noting that he is not addressing the full complement of the legion. Men have been seconded by the governor, detachments have reinforced other units and troops are posted across the province.

The wide-ranging deployment of troops is most apparent in the papyrus which records the different duties in which specific men serving in Egypt were involved – assisting with the grain supply, dredging the harbour, manufacturing papyri, working at the mint and assisting with the river patrol.

The duty rosters recorded in the Vindolanda writing tablets also stress the range of activities in which the soldiers were employed – shoemaking, building, plastering, clay-collecting.

The military unit aimed to be self-sufficient in many respects, as Vegetius emphasizes, and had its own craftsmen and skilled labour. But the sphere of interest ranged beyond the army base. Jobs such as policing and providing guards for the tax collectors were an extension of military duties. But other aspects such as harbour-dredging and building activities emphasize that the military units were often a good source of labour with skills that could benefit the local community.

Goodman, in stressing that much of the Roman army did little fighting, campaigning or defending, creates the impression, perhaps inadvertently, that the army was idle, when the evidence suggests that the life of the troops was a busy, varied and active one. This issue of the day-to-day duties of soldiers is important because it may have had an impact on recruitment and the appeal of a military career. Evidence for the mechanisms of army recruitment is meagre, especially the relative proportions in the ranks of conscripts and volunteers. Goodman mentions that conscription was a real fear for the inhabitants of the empire (Goodman, p.86) but many troops would have volunteered for service.

Exercise

Now read Goodman, pages 113–22. What, according to Goodman, were the attractions of military life? Why did people join the army?

Discussion

It is possible to identify several pragmatic reasons why men might choose to join the army. The most tangible of these is the regular pay (Goodman, p.118). In addition to their wages, the troops could expect to receive occasional gifts of money, for example, at an emperor's succession or to mark a great victory. The benefits of a steady income should not be underestimated since employment for the free-born population of the empire was often precarious. The army also offered opportunities for social advancement. This is most

auxillaries - joined as non-citizens -
retired as citizens

scope & promotion
commanding posts
senatorial + equestrian orders -
rank-+-file cld.
promote to centurion

legal privileges

apparent among the auxiliary soldiers, most of whom entered the ranks as non-citizens and left as citizens on their retirement. (For the advantages conveyed by citizenship, see Essay Five, 'Status and identity in the Roman world', which you met in Block Two.) All units of the army also offered considerable scope for promotion with associated increases in pay and prestige. The commanding posts in both legions and auxiliary units were occupied by members of the senatorial and equestrian orders but the rank-and-file soldier could still aspire to be a centurion (Goodman, pp.118–19). By comparison, few civilian jobs offered any sort of career ladder. A military career also conveyed certain legal privileges; not that soldiers were above abusing their advantaged position.

Soldiering a way
of life
self contained community
proud of history,
regimental pride

born into military

Apart from the practical benefits of a military career there may have been more emotive reasons which appealed to some recruits. Being a soldier was more than just a job, it was a whole way of life. Each legion and auxiliary unit could act as a self-contained community. Soldiers were encouraged to identify with their units and to be proud of their history; Goodman equates this to 'regimental pride' (Goodman, pp.114–15). The self-containment of the unit may have been compounded by local recruitment (if indeed this was ever a reality – see below); some men may have been born into military families and have had few career choices. For others, discipline, routine and security may have appealed. Goodman suggests that military life was not unpleasant. There were few risks to life and arbitrary postings were unusual (Goodman, pp.116–17). The sense of comradeship and community among the men may have compensated for reduced family ties although at least some soldiers formed lasting relationships and raised families. After service, the military still provided a support network; veterans would receive a retirement pay-off and could settle, if desired, in a military colony (Goodman, pp.120–21).

after service/support
network for veterans

rewarding
tough
marked decline in
recruits of troops
from Italy (1 AD)
thro' 1 AD
Praetorian
guard elite

It may be true to say that once a Roman soldier, always a Roman soldier, and that the military did well in looking after its own. Yet it is difficult to weigh up objectively the pros and cons of military life and to class it as a safe and pleasant option, or, indeed, vice versa. Military life could be rewarding but military life could also be tough. One piece of evidence does, however, militate against the army as a popular choice for all. This is the marked decline in recruitment of troops from Italy itself during the course of the first century AD. This may partially be explained by the development of the Praetorian Guard as an élite force recruited predominately from the Italian peninsula but it also suggests that for those living at the heart of the empire, extended service on the frontiers did not appeal; the disadvantages simply outweighed the advantages.

3.2 The identity of the Romano-British soldier

Throughout its Roman history, Britain maintained a substantial military presence. Tracing the history of this garrison is complex; military policy and aims are not always apparent, and even establishing which units were present in the island and where they were based can be difficult. Diverse sources can be drawn upon: literary references to campaigns, for example in the works of Tacitus; archaeological remains of forts and defences; *diplomata* (the discharge certificates of retired soldiers); writing tablets which record soldiers' activities, supply needs and personal correspondence; and inscriptions which record soldiers as builders, worshippers and commemorators of the dead. Piecing the evidence together provides an outline of the role of the army in Britain and some insights into the life of the soldiers.

In this section you will focus in particular on the identity of Romano-British soldiers. Who served in the army, and from where were they recruited? For your work in this section you will require the Illustrations Book, the offprints and Supplementary Texts. You will also watch a sequence on video cassette 2.

The deployment of troops in Roman Britain

The Roman army by its sheer overall scale may have served as an instrument to suppress internal dissent, but in Britain its immediate role was the conquest of the island and the maintenance, once it was established, of the northern frontier. Yet the nature and extent of the military presence in Britain was constantly affected by both internal and external threats elsewhere in the empire. The four legions which made up the initial invasion force were *legio II Augusta*, *legio IX Hispana*, *legio XIV Gemina* and *legio XX*. Numerous auxiliary units were probably also involved although few of their titles are known. The garrison was reduced to three legions in AD 66 when *legio XIV Gemina* was withdrawn in preparation for campaigns planned elsewhere by Nero. Detachments and auxiliary units were probably also withdrawn during the course of the civil war in AD 69. Under Vespasian the garrison was brought up to strength by the arrival of *legio II Adiutrix* and additional auxiliary forces. But Domitian's campaigns in Germany later forced the withdrawal of *legio II Adiutrix*. Under Trajan the *legio IX Hispana* was probably withdrawn for the emperor's campaigns in Parthia. Hadrian increased the legionary force to three again by the introduction of *legio VI Victrix* and three legions remained in the island until the fourth century.

Figure 4.4 *Fragment of a gravestone (?) showing three legionary soldiers from Croy Hill, Dumbartonshire, probably second century. National Museum of Antiquities, Scotland (By permission of the National Museums of Scotland)*

Legionary detachments were frequently called for service elsewhere, however, and the number of auxiliary troops also continued to fluctuate.

The soldiers were at the vanguard of the Roman presence in Britain and this must have been most apparent in the years immediately following the invasion and as the troops reached new bases. The constant presence of the army did not mean that the whole island was a continual military zone. With the advance of the army, old camps were abandoned and new ones founded (see Plates 4.19 and 4.20). By the early second century the army was increasingly concentrated in the west and north of the province and bases were becoming more fixed. *Legio II Augusta* was based in Exeter, then Gloucester (Plate 4.19) and from the Flavian period onwards made Caerleon in south Wales its home (Plate 4.20). *Legio IX*

(handwritten margin notes:) legionary detachments for elsewhere + auxiliary troops fluctuated

early (2 army mvr. conc. w+n + bases more fixed

Hispana was initially at Longthorpe, then Lincoln and then York (Plate 4.19) before its withdrawal from the island. *Legio XIV Gemina* initially operated in the Midlands and was then based at Wroxeter before its withdrawal. *Legio XX* occupied the bases of Colchester, Kingsholm, Usk and Wroxeter (Plate 4.19) before settling at Chester (Plate 4.20). As the situation in the island, at least in the south, became more stable and the northern advance was halted, the bases of the legions became static. Thus when *legio VI Victrix* arrived under Hadrian it moved straight to York and remained there (Plate 4.20). Tracing the whereabouts and movements of the many auxiliary units which served in Britain is more problematic, although by the second century many were concentrated in the region of Hadrian's Wall (Plate 4.20). The majority of military camps may have become permanent but this did not mean that the troops were stationary, since detachments might be called to serve anywhere in the island and also in other provinces.

[handwritten margin notes: stability; static bases; by C2 many in region Hadrian's wall]

Soldiers and civilians

Wherever they were based, the soldiers were the representatives of Rome; the troops served the Roman emperor and they symbolized the Roman power and presence in the island. The soldiers were outsiders because they were military men rather than civilians and because they were Romans rather than natives (although see below for discussion of the diverse origins of troops); distinctions which may have been felt most acutely when the army first arrived in a new area. It is difficult to reconstruct the degree of interaction between the Roman army and the civil population, and the impact that the arrival of the troops may have made. It is worth remembering the sheer scale of the army. For example there were 5,000–6,000 men in each legion and the presence of such a unit may have had a major impact on the economy and society of the areas where they were stationed. In some circumstances trouble could flare up. It was noted earlier that soldiers could abuse their authority (Goodman, pp.121–2) and in general the troops, especially *en masse*, may have seemed menacing and intimidating. One of the problems which apparently led to the revolt of Boudicca was the poor relationship between soldiers and civilians.

[handwritten margin notes: soldiers reps of Rome syms Roman power; impact of army on civil pop unknown – interaction – unknown how much; 5,000–6,000 men in a legion; abuse authority; menacing + intimidating in numbers]

Exercise

Turn now to Tacitus' account of the revolt of Boudicca, reproduced as extract 4.3 in the Supplementary Texts. Read paragraphs 31–32.

What part did the soldiers and veterans allegedly play in antagonizing the native Britons?

Discussion

The abuses which occurred to the family of the dead king Prasutagus, according to Tacitus, involved the army. The kingdom was plundered by centurions, suggesting unruly and uncontrolled military behaviour and implying that one of the prizes or rewards of military service was booty. In Colchester the military was also a cause of resentment. To make way for the veterans, native people had been displaced and in the process insulted. The Roman settlers acted arrogantly, viewing themselves as superior to the British 'prisoners and slaves'. The serving soldiers were little better and looked forward to the day when they could act as badly. Tacitus may be simplifying events surrounding the revolt; after all, he was not above championing the cause of the noble native over the negative sides of Roman imperialism (as you will see again in Block Five). Nevertheless the implication is that army abuses were perceived as a contributory factor to the British unrest.

The abusiveness and arrogance of troops may have soured relations between the military and civilian elements of the population, but some of the tension probably had its origins not in what the soldiers did, but in what they stood for. Note how Tacitus plays up the contrasts of Roman versus native and the military versus civilian in the events leading up to the revolt of Boudicca. Despite the picture which Tacitus paints, Camulodunum was not just a military settlement; it contained civilians as well as retired soldiers. Tacitus refers to the presence of women and old people. Wives, children, and no doubt others who provided essential services, inhabited the settlement. It would be unlikely that all these people were immigrants. In addition, the 'Romanness' of those soldiers and veterans who found themselves in Britain following the invasion could also be questioned. These men were the representatives of Rome and the invading power and were thus in the broadest sense 'Roman'. But the label suggests some sort of homogeneity in terms of background and experience which may have been lacking. Without detailed personal records it is impossible to assert exactly where soldiers serving in Britain or elsewhere originated from. Inscriptions, however, sometimes refer to the *origo* or town of origin for named soldiers. Unfortunately the epigraphic record for Britain is limited but those inscriptions which do include the origins of the soldiers suggest that although some were from Italy, others were from Gaul, Thrace, Germany and other provinces (discussed further below). It is also known that before the invasion, the legions had been stationed for relatively long periods elsewhere; for example *legio II Augusta*, *legio XIV Gemina* and *legio XX* had all been in Germany for thirty years. These legions may have attracted some local recruits or brought camp followers with them when they arrived in

Britain. As for the auxiliary troops, who must have formed a substantial part of the initial invasion force, these were by definition originally enlisted in the provinces. All this leads to the question of how Roman the Roman army really was. Many of the soldiers may have been representatives of a place they had never visited and representatives of an emperor they had never seen.

So how did the legionaries and auxiliaries perceive themselves in relation to Rome, the army and the Britons? One method of considering this issue is to look at some of the monuments and inscriptions which were set up to and by members of the army. What types of language, both verbal and pictorial, are employed to describe different groups of people?

You will be asked in a moment to watch video cassette 2, sequence 2, *VC2* 'Text and image on tombstones'. This video sequence complements the audio cassette band on reading inscriptions, which you studied in Block Two. You may wish to listen to the audio cassette band again, and refer back to the related notes, before proceeding.

As you work through the video sequence, you will need to have to hand Plates 4.17, 4.18 and 4.21 in the Illustrations Book, and will need *tombstone inscriptions* to refer to the transcriptions and translations of the tombstones illustrated there, given below.

The aim of the video sequence is to note some common elements of funerary inscriptions and the language used in epitaphs to describe and define people. You will look at the epitaphs in context in order to understand how each monument communicated as an integrated whole. The video begins by considering the nature and role of the Roman cemetery by exploring evidence from Pompeii. Three Romano-British tombstones are then studied in detail.

The text of the inscriptions is given below. Three versions of each inscription are provided. Version (a) reproduces, as closely as possible, the original form and layout of the inscription. Version (b) decodes the inscription, filling out any abbreviations, and version (c) provides a translation. These texts are provided for reference. In this exercise I want to focus on the context of the inscriptions, so please try to read as much as you can from the tombstones themselves. For this purpose you may find it useful to pause the video at key moments, or to refer to the plates.

Exercise

Watch video cassette 2, sequence 2 (t.c.19:09–42:39) now.

The tombstone of Marcus Favonius Facilis, Colchester (t.c.23:43, Plate 4.17)

(a) M FAVON M F POL FACI
   LIS LEG XX VERECVND
   VS ET NOVICIVS LIB POSV
   ERVNT H S E

(b) M(arcus) FAVON(ius) M(arci) F(ilius) POL(lia tribu) FACI/LIS
   (Centurio) LEG(ionis) XX VERECVND/VS
   ET NOVICIVS LIB(erti) POSV/ERVNT
   H(ic) S(itus) E(st)

(c) Marcus Favonius Facilis, son of Marcus of the Pollia voting-tribe,
   centurion of the Twentieth Legion. The freed slaves Verecundus and
   Novicius set this up. He lies here.

The tombstone of the auxiliary cavalryman Longinus, Colchester (t.c.31:02, Plate 4.18)

(a) LONGINVS SDAPEZE
   MATYCI F DVPLICARIVS
   ALA PRIMA TRACVM PAGO
   SARDI ANNO XL AEROR XV
   HEREDES EXS TESTAM C
   H S E

(b) LONGINVS SDAPEZE
   MATYCI F(ilius) DVPLICARIVS
   ALA PRIMA TRACVM PAGO
   SARDI(ca) ANNO(rum) XL AEROR(um) XV
   HEREDES EXS TESTAM(ento) C(uraverunt)
   H(ic) S(itus) E(st)

(c) Longinus Sdapeze son of Matycus [or Longinus son of
   Sdapezematycus], a duplicarius of the First unit of Thracian Cavalry
   from the district of Sardica, aged 40 with 15 years' service. His heirs
   had this set up according to the terms of his will. He lies here.

The tombstone of Regina, Arbeia, South Shields (t.c.37:33, Plate 4.21)

(a) DM REGINA LIBERTA ET CONIVGE
   BARATES PALMYRENVS NATIONE
   CATVALLAVNA AN XXX

(b) D(is) M(anibus) REGINA LIBERTA ET CONIVGE
   BARATES PALMYRENVS NATIONE
   CATVALLAVNA AN(norum) XXX

(c) To the spirits of the departed. Regina, a freedwoman and wife, a Catuvellaunian, aged 30. Barates of Palmyra (set this up).

[Beneath, in Palmyrene:] Regina, the freedwoman of Barates, alas.

Furthur references

For further images of tombstones, refer to the following illustrations:

Plates 4.22 and 4.23 in the Illustrations Book: images of two military tombstones from Roman Britain;

Plate 0.2: the military tombstone which was discussed in the Introduction to the Course;

Block One, Figure 1.4 (p.81): the tombstone from the German fort of Mainz, showing a soldier carrying a military standard;

Essay Five, Figure 5.2 (p.133): a further Mainz tombstone.

Britons in the Roman Army

Tombstones from Roman Britain are often suggestive of mixed and complex identities for those commemorated and those acting as commemorators. The monuments are Roman in form, inscribed with Latin epitaphs and adorned with pictures that celebrate Roman values. The tombstones often indicate that those commemorated were outsiders in Britain, such as soldiers who were distant from their homelands. Yet in some cases, although they are commemorated by Roman-style monuments, those recorded were not even Roman citizens. These individuals were doubly outsiders; they were neither native or Roman but were between the conquered and the conquerors.

The Roman army itself was full of distinctions of status which were further reinforced by the gradations of rank present in the army's complex hierarchical structure. Despite this mixing of cultures and status, the Roman army was unified rather than divided. Men of diverse backgrounds and status were united behind the standards of Rome and shared a common identity as soldiers. The army created a sense of belonging which could be reinforced by the individual soldier's identification with his unit of service. The legionary or auxiliary unit could stand as a self-contained community meeting the practical and emotional needs of its members; it fed, clothed and employed its men and provided them with comrades and mutual support networks. At death the soldiers were defined in military terms: rank, unit and years of service were the facts of their life often recorded in detail by their fellow soldiers. The role of the military unit or camp as a society within a society has important implications for the maintenance of the discipline of the troops. Loyalty to the unit and the military meant by association loyalty to the commander-in-chief of the army: the emperor. For the soldier his life was proscribed by the military regime and service to the emperor. The ideal was that all other identities – civilian, provincial and familial – were subsumed to the military identity. The men were first and foremost soldiers, and all else was secondary to this. Nevertheless beneath the surface the ideal was often subverted; the soldiers were not a homogenous mass, and the tombstones at least hint at some of the inequalities and uncertainties faced by those who served Rome, distant from their homelands or among hostile populations or without the benefits of citizenship.

The majority of the memorials so far considered date from the first and early second century AD when the army was a relatively new presence in Britain. Did the situation remain the same? Were the soldiers always regarded as outsiders? And was the military community always so distinct from the civilian community? To answer these questions it is necessary to establish where the soldiers serving in Britain came from. The difficulties of tracing recruitment patterns for individual military units has already been noted. This has not, however, prevented scholars exploring the extent to which outsiders and Britons came to man the British garrison.

Exercise

You will read in a moment offprint 4.3, which is an extract taken from an article by Dobson and Mann. This article examines the evidence for the service of Britons in the Roman army, both in Britain itself and elsewhere in the empire. The extract comes from the end of the article, and explores the role of Britons in the legions. Please note that the extract contains many footnotes. In general these refer to inscriptions, and sometimes other evidence, which support the specific points being made. You should not be intimidated by the Latin text and unit titles found in the footnotes, and occasionally in the text, since you are not expected to be able to translate or remember this information.

Please read offprint 4.3 now. What evidence do Dobson and Mann employ to support their arguments about local recruitment?

Discussion

In the extract Dobson and Mann explore the available evidence for the service of Britons in the Roman army, especially their service in Britain itself. Prior to this extract they consider recruitment to auxiliary units, and despite the lack of specific evidence Dobson and Mann believe it likely that Britons were recruited into the auxiliary units stationed in the province. Recruitment into the citizen-based

[handwritten margin note: NB Dobson Mann Romano – Brit army locally recruited]

[handwritten margin note: likely Brits recruited to auxiliary units stationed in province.]

legions is considered next. Dobson and Mann employ *origines* as recorded in inscriptions to assess whether Britons, especially from the colonies founded in Britain, were recruited. Service in Britain by British legionaries is rarely attested but Dobson and Mann suggest of legionary tombstones with no *origo* that 'many of these must be Britons'. The basis for this claim is evidence from other provinces which suggests that local recruitment had become the norm by the mid second century. Dobson and Mann accept the extreme paucity of the British evidence but argue from comparison with trends in other provinces that local recruits probably staffed the auxiliary units and legions of Britain. To sum up, there are two main types of evidence used by Dobson and Mann: direct evidence mainly from inscriptions (although some discharge diplomas and literary references are also relevant); and comparative evidence drawn from other provinces where local recruitment was practised.

The conclusion of Dobson and Mann that the British garrison was locally recruited is important because of the impact such a policy would have had on the make-up of the army and its interaction with the civil community. If the soldiers were locally recruited, and especially if they came to be born and bred in the settlements surrounding military forts, this would have negated many of the potential differences between soldiers and civilians. The military would no longer be outsiders but overwhelmingly part of the local community with considerable familial ties within the province. It is worth emphasizing that under the early empire, soldiers were not allowed to marry. But unofficial liaisons were often tolerated although any dependants probably lived outside the forts in civil settlements. Indeed it has been the investigation of the familial relationships of Romano-British soldiers which has led to a major challenge to the position advocated by Dobson and Mann.

Exercise

You should next read offprint 4.4, an extract taken from an article by Saller and Shaw. This article involves a statistical analysis of the familial relationships recorded in Latin epitaphs from the western provinces of the empire. Saller and Shaw are particularly interested in family structure and note the widespread prevalence of the recording of relationships from within the nuclear family. Some areas such as Britain, however, diverge from this pattern. The extract explores possible reasons why.

Read offprint 4.4 now. How and why do Saller and Shaw challenge the view that the Romano-British army was locally recruited?

Discussion

Saller and Shaw focus on a type of evidence extensively exploited by Dobson and Mann – tombstones. Saller and Shaw, however, are interested in the familial content of the epitaphs rather than statements of origin. In a wide-ranging study, Saller and Shaw analyse the relationships between the deceased person and the person who acted as commemorator and use this evidence to make assertions about the structure of the Roman family. In considering military epitaphs, Saller and Shaw are struck by differences in the types of commemorator found among military populations. Among the British military, in contrast with some other provinces, few members of the family acted as commemorators to soldiers; instead friends and non-kin heirs set up tombstones. Saller and Shaw take this as evidence that there was a low level of family formation among soldiers stationed in Britain. This is then related to army recruitment. If soldiers were recruited in Britain they would have been more likely to be commemorated by members of their family, whereas the lack of familial references in the epitaphs suggest that the men were born outside the province. Saller and Shaw reassess the evidence that was previously employed to support the view that recruitment was local. The direct evidence for Britons serving in Britain is meagre, and Saller and Shaw consider that the comparative evidence employed by Dobson and Mann entails too many assumptions. Saller and Shaw do not believe that just because local recruitment was a reality elsewhere in the empire, the same can be assumed to apply in Britain. Thus they reach the opposite conclusion: that the troops serving in Britain were imported from other provinces.

The conclusions of Dobson and Mann and Saller and Shaw diverge sharply and illustrate how similar evidence can be interpreted differently when it explicitly supports neither point of view. I will leave it up to you which set of arguments you prefer or find more convincing. However, it is worth noting a few points. First of all, consider the nature of the evidence employed. Both sides extensively exploit inscriptions although the epigraphic record from Britain is meagre. Saller and Shaw speak of the tombstone data with confidence, yet the number of tombstones available from Roman Britain is insignificant compared with those of other provinces. Secondly, it is worth noting that chronology is key to the arguments of both sides since both explore whether the source of recruits to the British garrison changed across time. Yet Saller and Shaw make no attempt to date any of the tombstones they utilize; Dobson and Mann do note that the evidence becomes more sparse with time but do not explain why this happened. Thirdly, you may also want to think

Figure 4.5 *Line drawing of a votive pillar from Maryport, inscribed* Roman Aeternae et Fortunae Reduci *['To Eternal Rome and to Fortune who takes us back home']. From Collingwood and Wright, 1965, no.840. (By permission of the Administrators of the Haverfield Bequest)*

more closely about what is meant by the term 'local recruitment'. In both articles there is a general failure to distinguish between recruits drawn from the immediate environs of military forts and those drawn from the island overall. Would a man born and bred in Gloucester or Colchester think himself serving locally if he was posted to Hadrian's Wall?

The question of whether large numbers of Britons came to serve in the army in Britain remains unanswered, and unless new evidence is uncovered it will probably never be resolved. This is frustrating in terms of building a picture of life in the province, especially in the frontier zone, and exploring issues such as the extent to which the native population interacted with the military. Nevertheless it seems possible to make some general observations. With time the major military bases became permanent; civilians would have become accustomed to the military presence whether the soldiers were locally recruited or not. Civilian settlements developed around the army bases, feeding off the soldiers economically and socially. In the next section you will explore some of these interactions and relationships in more detail. At this point it is sufficient to note that as the native population came to tolerate, depend on and integrate with the military presence, the differences between soldiers and civilians probably declined. After all, whether the soldiers were British or not, most of them, unless they were sent on detachments elsewhere, would have served at the same post for twenty years and may have chosen to settle in

over time
major military bases became permanent

civilian settlements dev'd round army base

soldiers based in areas
for long time - retire there

the area on retirement. This permanency would have given the soldiers adequate opportunity to establish liaisons with local women and have families if they so wished. If these families are not recorded in the epitaphs this may suggest no more than the possibility that the act of inscribing epitaphs was never extensively adopted. The soldiers, wherever they were recruited from, continued to be the representatives of Rome in Britain, but with time the stark differences between the military and civilian population declined.

Summing up: multiple identities

At the beginning of this part of the block, it was noted that the army was the power base of the emperor; its sheer scale guaranteed the emperor's safety. In speaking, however, of the size of the Roman army and hundreds of thousands of troops, it is easy to lose sight of the soldier as an individual. In this section and the previous section, however, I have tried to highlight some of the issues which must have been personal to each soldier. Who were the troops? Why did they join the army? Where did they come from? The successful projection of a common Roman military identity often obscures the answers to such questions. The individual soldier becomes a military statistic. This is well illustrated by the military tombstones, where standard language and standard images reflect the regimented lives of those commemorated. Yet sometimes it is possible to sense that although military identity was paramount, other identities and roles were not completely obscured. As the tombstones of Regina and Barates suggest, it was possible to be involved with the army and also a family; it was possible to be Roman but also British and Palmyrene. The soldiers of the Roman army, like so many inhabitants of the empire, often had complex social identities.

3.3   Frontier culture: military and civilian in northern Britain

In the parts of first-century Britain which you have considered so far, you have seen the immediate effects of Roman invasion and the Boudiccan revolt, and how these events, so directly concerned with the taking of power, were closely tied in with questions of identity. Obviously there are many ways in which these events can be – and were at the time – interpreted oppositionally: 'Romans' and 'Britons', 'them' and 'us'. But in your work on the army as much as on local communities in Britain you will have noticed that these divisions were not so clear cut, and became less so once initial conflicts were past. For instance, there was the matter of British recruitment into the army, an army which you have seen had a 'Roman' identity of a rather particular kind. Then in the towns there was the matter of the Romanization of the local élites, who

divisions not clear
British recruitment
in an army with a
'Roman' identity
towns - Romanization
of élite locals

came to use aspects of the imported lifestyle to assert their own status. It becomes much less meaningful to talk of distinctive cultures, 'Roman' and 'British', when we look closely and critically at the evidence, especially from the late first century AD on.

We turn now to look at an area of Britain which provides a rather particular context for the interactions of culture, identity and power. This is the frontier area of southern Scotland and northern England, which was the northern limit of the Roman empire.

Frontier zones often have rather different cultures from the central areas of their territory. By definition they are places 'at the edge', where some kind of border (marked or unmarked) separates one area from another. Sometimes this borderline relates to features of the terrain such as mountains or rivers, which offer natural boundary limits, but often it is the result of some decisive human activity. Then it may mark the place where one particular culture ends, even where 'civilization' peters out. Or it may be heavily contested by forces on each side so that its very location becomes a matter of contention and conflict.

For such reasons, frontier areas tend to miss out on many aspects of the culture enjoyed in places more centrally situated: they have different patterns of settlement and communication and their people have different concerns and opportunities. Life may be harder and sparser, with people used to managing outside a central support system and involved perhaps in various trans-frontier operations. On the other hand, the frontier situation often generates a culture of its own. This is particularly so when troops are brought in to protect it. The military presence brings its own institutional culture as well as that of its individual personnel. In addition, it attracts other people to the area to service the army camps with professional goods and food and clothing. All this brings about new communities and communications in the area where various cultures interact together around the frontier line: military and civilian, locals and outsiders mix together in ways which may not happen in more central parts of the territory.

The British frontier of the Roman empire demonstrates all these features. As you may remember from the brief discussion of the empire and its limits that occurs in the Introduction to the Course (if not, look back at it now), the concept of boundary was integral to a view of empire. Questions of where and why Roman power (the ambivalent word *imperium*) would find its limits were important ones, not just in the territorial policies of different emperors, but also for how they were used to articulate issues of culture inside and outside the Roman empire. What lay within their control represented to the Romans the known and familiar; but what lay outside could be presented as strange and different, with the potential to strengthen or subvert what Romans felt about themselves. As David Braund explained in his interview on Tacitus

[handwritten margin notes: frontiers 'at the edge'; edge of 'civilization'; frontiers - diff patterns - settlemt + comm. - people diff. concerns + opps; trans-frontier operations; frontier culture attracts people to service camps; new communities + communications; concept 'boundary'; known + familiar; strange + diff.]

David Braund
'exotic' conquest motive

Britain - legendary remoteness

Brit. lay across 'Monster-filled ocean' Horace

Suetonius Gaius 'spoils' - shells

Claudius 'conquered Ocean'

VC2.3

Jones' 3-level approach observables (relationships) inferences

and Britain (audio cassette 4, band 1) extending their 'civilizing rule' over such places represented a challenge that was not simply military: exploring the exotic and bringing it within the bounds of empire was presented as a powerful motive for conquest.

This was particularly the case with Britain because of its legendary remoteness. Augustan poets linked Britain with visions of great empire as it was a marginal place *par excellence*: to bring Britain into the empire would 'make Augustus a god on earth' (Horace *Odes* 3.5.2–3). But the challenge – and the prize, perhaps – was made greater by the fact that Britain lay across the sea, the 'monster-filled Ocean' as Horace *Odes* 4.14.47–8 described it. This was a theme also taken up by historians, who wrote about various attempts at conquest: according to Suetonius (*Gaius* 48), the emperor Gaius (Caligula), after his abortive attempt at crossing, had his soldiers take home shells as 'spoils from Ocean owed to the Capitol and Palatine', while the successful Claudius set up special trophies in Rome in his triumphal celebrations 'as a sign that he had crossed and, as it were, conquered Ocean' (Suetonius, *Claudius* 17). So, in conquering the Ocean, the boundary set by nature, the Romans gained access to Britain, and thus gained the opportunity of pushing the boundaries of their empire even further north.

Video cassette 2, sequence 3 (which covers a period of about 120 years from the 80s AD to the early third century) concentrates on two aspects of this. First, it looks at where and why this northern boundary stopped where it did, and why its location shifted on various occasions. As you will see, there are reasons for believing that the original Roman vision was to conquer the whole of the island of Britain but the Romans withdrew their military forces from the north of Scotland, thus creating the need to demarcate a particular limit to their power. Where this boundary was drawn – in the corridor of land between the Tyne and Solway, and then briefly between the Forth and the Clyde – frontier areas developed where the Roman military and local civilian cultures met. This meeting and exchange of cultures is the second focus. Remembering Jones's three-level approach to using archaeological data, look out for material which shows the kinds of relationships that existed between these different groups as you watch.

In this video sequence you will hear some opinions expressed about how these various borderlines (the Stanegate line, Hadrian's Wall, and the Antonine Wall) may have functioned as frontiers at different times. As you watch, you will need to think about what kind of functions a frontier may fulfil, from defensive barrier to crossing control or symbolic statement. Look back, too, at the list of dates you made in your study of section 2.1 of this block (based on Goodman, pp.208–11, should you want to cross-check) for the dates of Agricola's campaigns in Scotland and for the building and occupation of the two walls.

You may find it useful to refer to the map of Britain in Goodman on page 210, which shows the course of both walls, and to the following illustrations:

Plate 4.24: a diagram of a cross-section through Hadrian's Wall (showing the relative positions of wall, ditches, and *vallum*);

Plate 4.25: a plan of Poltross Burn milecastle, which you see on the video at t.c.49:40;

Plate 4.1: the fort at Arbeia, showing some typical features in its plan.

In the video, reference is also made to the following literary sources:

On Hadrian's Wall: 'Hadrian was the first to build a wall, eighty miles long to separate the Romans from the barbarians' (*Augustan History: Hadrian* 11.2);

On the Antonine Wall: 'For he (Antoninus Pius) conquered the Britons too, through the governor Lollius Urbicus, and after driving back the barbarians he built a second wall of turf' (*Augustan History: Antoninus Pius*).

Please now watch video cassette 2, sequence 3, 'Rome's British frontiers' (t.c.42:44–1:19:01).

√ c 2·3

Exercise

How does the archaeological material shown in this video sequence support the views expressed? Are there other interpretations which might also be valid?

Discussion

In this discussion I will look at each of the frontiers in turn and consider the evidence presented and its possible interpretation. It is important to remember that some of the interpretations depend on more detailed evidence than we could refer to in the video: for instance, close studies of pottery, as you saw at Arbeia, can help to date the occupation of forts, while pollen analysis has shown that north of Hadrian's Wall there was a greater amount of grassland and to the south more cultivation of cereal (thus opening up questions about the ecology of the frontier). Once again, many detailed pieces of evidence go towards building up the picture of this frontier territory.

Dick Whittaker's comments (beginning at t.c.44:16) on the notions of frontier provide an ideological context. They obviously relate to work you have just done in the block about boundaries and boundlessness in the Roman empire, but also tie in, I would suggest, with the Roman attitude to Scotland (which Goodman

boundaries/
boundlessness

Roman attitude
to Scotland

border in northern Engld set a limit to empire

scottish view of frontiers in Brit - pos. - retreat i barriers i launching points i

describes on p.211 as 'ambivalent'). The total conquest of Scotland (which may have been Agricola's aim in the 80s AD) would have demonstrated the Romans' unconquerability, while a border in northern England obviously reflected the need to set a limit to their empire. Seeing the sequence of frontiers in Britain in a Scottish context can give a helpful perspective on purpose and function: were they positions of retreat to which Romans repaired after failing to hold parts of Scotland, or barriers against barbarians from the north, or launching points for renewed campaigns in Scotland? All of these interpretations have relevance. It is also important to think about the areas more immediately to the north of these frontiers and how they and their inhabitants were affected. An interesting factor here is that none of these frontiers seems to have followed a local tribal boundary, and in that sense they did not start as cultural borders; in fact at its western end Hadrian's Wall actually bisected a tribal territory.

The Stanegate line

strategic supply road then line - forts

As Lindsay Allason-Jones describes (beginning at t.c.46:34), this early frontier seems to have had two rather different lives. First it was built as a strategic supply road to support the Roman troops in Scotland, and then, when they retreated back to this area, it received a line of forts. She assesses it, in this later stage, as 'a frontier in the sense that it was where the province stopped' (t.c.47:07) but not as a defensive barrier against the enemy. Obviously the prime evidence for this lies in the material remains of the road system and in the forts (although the precise dating of some of these is hard to establish). Further remarkable evidence for the life of these forts, both military and social, has come from the artefacts preserved in Vindolanda, in particular the fragments of wooden writing tablets (t.c.1:14:58) and luxury goods such as the examples you saw in the video (t.c.1:05:29). (It is clear from some of the military archives that are preserved just how important supplies were to the Roman army at the frontiers, and this opens up a whole range of economic factors relevant to civilians and soldiers that the video had no space to deal with.) A rather different kind of evidence for the Stanegate line being to some extent a natural frontier is its geographical location between the River Tyne and Solway Firth.

Vindolanda. wooden writing tablets

supplies impt to soldiers - interesting at frontiers - economic factors

defensive purpose

Other interpretations may consider the degree to which the line of forts served a defensive purpose. Were they just a convenient home for the army withdrawn from Scotland, or was there a real need to defend the locality against attackers of its own? Or was it, perhaps, less a case of defence, but more of general control and surveillance? Certainly the area did have defensive needs of its own, as can be deduced from the decision to build Hadrian's Wall: presumably the Stanegate line had cease to meet them.

Hadrian's Wall

The situation around the building of Hadrian's Wall is complicated because of the various changes of building plan that seem to have occurred in its earliest years. It is important both to understand the individual pieces of evidence and interpret the wider picture. (Think back to Jones's three stages in offprint 4.1.)

In the video it is generally suggested that Hadrian's Wall was originally intended to improve the control of the area, and that certain defensive aspects were then increased. Conceptually, for the Romans it may have been seen as a culturally defining frontier.

These general statements obviously depend on a wide array of evidence. The route chosen for the wall, which took advantage of the craggy terrain, suggests enhanced surveillance and enhanced defensibility as an aim. The most important indication that defence became a greater priority is the move to accommodate soldiers in forts built on the wall itself. Forts with access on to the territory north of the wall were obviously intended to facilitate Roman troop movements in that direction, again suggesting that there were attacks to be repulsed. The second building phase also limited the amount of through-traffic across the wall by the construction of the *vallum* (which also increased protection behind the wall on the southern side). It cut off access via the north–south gates in the numerous milecastles, channelling people through forts (such as Benwell; t.c.51:55). Yet despite this increased defensibility, it seems unlikely from its design and dimensions that the wall functioned as a continuous fighting-platform (in contrast with Rudyard Kipling's imaginative description of it in a much later phase, which you can see in extract 4.6).

There is other evidence to support this general view of control moving towards defence that is not from the immediate site of the wall (and was not mentioned in the video sequence). This comes from forts and fortifications in the wider vicinity which obviously stood in some functional relationship to the wall. To the north of the wall were several outlying forts (at Bewcastle, Netherby and Birrens) which were probably built at the time the wall was started, possibly to guard the territory of the Brigantes to the north of the wall. Along the Cumbrian coast there seems to have been a line of

[handwritten margin notes:]
gen. control & surveillance?

orig. intended improve control, area certain defensive aspects then increased

route – wall – enhanced surveillance " defensibility.

forts

Roman troop movements nec. repulse attacks

vallum – cut off access via N/S gates people channelled thro' forts

not a cont fighting platform

control moving towards defence

outlying forts

forts and fortifications (such as small forts and towers and stretches of ditch and palisade) which virtually continued the line of the wall. Some of the forts in this stretch are pre-Hadrianic (such as Maryport) which suggests that they were not necessarily begun as part of the overall plan.

Once again, other interpretations can be made of this evidence and are likely to hinge on matters of degree or definition: how permeable was the wall, and by whom? When does control become defence? Can such a barrier be seen as a frontier? Even so, you have seen some details which cannot easily be explained in the context of these issues. It is not clear why part of the wall was made of turf, or why the stone wall was initially planned to be so wide. Perhaps the reduction in size was an act of realism turning a wall that was meant to impress by size (a 'symbolic' boundary?) into something more functional. (An interesting indication that the wall was considered a notable monument in Roman Britain is provided by the so-called Rudge Cup, which depicts and names some of its forts in a schematized frieze; see Colour Plate 4.3.)

The Antonine Wall

It was suggested in the video that this wall may have been initiated for powerful political reasons, namely the emperor's need for a victory to impress people back in Rome (remember the 'need' for Claudius to conquer Britain in the first place). But it was also made clear that reasons for the wall's inception and abandonment twenty years later remain unclear: wider needs of empire may have been more important than local disturbances.

The evidence given for this is really limited here to sculptures, but the interviewee, Lawrence Keppie, is obviously drawing on knowledge of what was happening elsewhere in the empire to contextualize his interpretation of developments on the wall. In terms of material evidence, much has been lost through modern building along the wall, but again, close examination of finds can help to date when forts were built and later left. It is much harder to find evidence to explain why.

Amidst this uncertainty the sculpted distance slabs, with their Roman iconography of victory, do indeed seem to underline the symbolic value of the wall in Roman terms. They speak in Roman terms as if to an exclusively Roman audience. It appears to have been the case that many of the distance slabs were carefully dismantled by the Romans themselves before they withdrew, another sign perhaps of their high symbolic value.

The shortage of evidence on which to base a more satisfactory account of developments at the Antonine Wall makes it difficult to suggest any thorough-going alternative interpretation. In particular the uncertainty about the real extent of local unrest at this time prevents a fuller understanding of its defensive purpose: was it needed to push the enemy back further north? Or did it perhaps have a value protecting trade and supplies across the lowland areas of Scotland?

This discussion has obviously concentrated on material evidence and its interpretation; we have little historical evidence for specific events which must have stimulated some of the developments described. But its purpose has been to help you to try to unpick the relationship between evidence and interpretation, and to look at the range of possible readings.

To end your work on the frontier I want to raise some questions to do with art as evidence for acculturation, taking examples from the sphere of religion. Later on in Block Five you will be looking at some similar material from North Africa.

In the video sequence you saw many instances of Roman dedications to gods (t.c.1:06:56ff.), traditional and otherwise: in a military frontier area where cultural patterns often differed from those in the heart of the territory and where soldiers must have sought the help of whichever deity might support them, their range is not suprising. Yet many of the questions they open up have a wide application for interpreting provincial art and religion, particularly in terms of culture, identity and power. What follows is simply a brief indication of some possibilities and for that reason I have made some rather bold assertions which, of course, conceal a much more nuanced situation.

Firstly, there are questions concerning the expression of imperial power which can be examined through a range of examples. One important group relates to practices of 'official' cults brought by the army to this part of Britain. Some of these were relevant to the internal culture of the camp, such as the annual dedication of a new altar to show loyalty to the emperor. Plate 4.26 shows one of the remarkable series found at Maryport fort. But other examples relate more explicitly to a situation of Roman military victory in the area, such as the distance slab from Bridgeness on the Antonine Wall (Plate 4.27), depicting on one side an official sacrifice before action, and on the other the resulting Roman victory. This image obviously had some local significance, but its iconography was common in Roman official art across the empire (think back to the second part of sequence 2 on video cassette 1, 'The Emperor in the provinces'). These examples, then,

'global' Roman power

personifications

Britannia
Aphrodisias image
submitting to emp'
Claudius

suggest a 'global' Roman power which made no reference to the British location in which it was set. In contrast are personifications in which Romans embodied particular aspects of Britain in a classical iconography familiar to them. One is Britannia, whom you met earlier in this block in the Aphrodisias image (Plate 4.4) submitting to the emperor Claudius, and who now represents the province of Britannia incorporated within the Roman empire. Lawrence Keppie identified her (t.c.58:25) in the figure presiding benignly over the victorious Roman in a distance slab from the Antonine Wall (Plate 4.28), but perhaps more certain are the images on imperial coins. These vary the position of her figure to signify changes in the province's fortune and her implicit dependency on Rome: slumped in misery she appears in need of the emperor's intervention (see the coin of Hadrian: Plate 4.29), while with strength restored she sits serenely upright (see the coin of Britannia: Plate 4.30). If Britannia expresses Roman triumph in Britain, Brigantia (the local British tribal territory) is personified in terms of religious power. Dedicated by a military engineer (*architectus*), a relief found at the Roman fort of Birrens (Dumfriesshire) (Plate 4.31) depicts her with highly classical attributes: a mural crown shows she is protectress of her territory (compare the head of 'Asia' on the El Djem mosaic in Essay One, Figure 1.1), while the Gorgon's head and armour link her with Minerva, the wings with Victory and the globe with Juno-Caelestis (with whom she is also linked on the altar from Corbridge, as you saw in the video at t.c.1:16:57). Together, these elements make this a syncretistic image in which the spirit of the locality is linked with other major goddesses of the empire (you will see more of Caelestis in Block Five), perhaps suggesting some universal appeal.

NB

This image of Brigantia leads to a second question raised by images of local British deities: just how useful are they as primary evidence for native cult and culture (for which, as you realize by now, there is such limited information)? The essential difficulty in answering this is that such images have been mediated through Roman artistic expression. This was very clear in the relief of Brigantia which included so many classical attributes, but is also the case for the head of Antenociticus and even for the so-called *Genii Cucullati* (the three hooded figures on the relief from Housesteads shown in Figure 4.6; t.c.1:10:58). This mediation may perhaps seem less surprising when the images are of local deities appropriated by Romans ready to cross cultures in the hope of securing favours from the powerful gods. (You may like to look back at **Essay Nine**, 'Religion in the Roman empire', and Figure 9.1 for a comparable Roman dedication from Germany.) For their dedication they often needed an image of the god, as you have seen for Cocidius (on the silver plaques; t.c.1:13:17) and Antenociticus (the fragments of sculpture from the shrine at Benwell: t.c.1:12:10). But had the locals necessarily

influence of local dress based on Burgh hooded cloaks

fertility symbolism poss.

Figure 4.6 *Relief showing the* Genii Cucullati *from the* vicus. *Housesteads Museum (By permission of English Heritage)*

envisaged these gods in these particular forms? One way of approaching this is to look for 'Roman' and 'local' elements. For instance, the images of Cocidius may be very schematized but they clearly show warrior attributes, like the Roman Mars. The head of Antenociticus owes much more to local influences in terms of stylistic treatment (of the eyes and hair for instance) and the attributes of tiny horns and a torc of which fragments remain around the neck; yet the very concept of a cult statue like this is Roman. For other representations (outside the context of Roman dedication) there is a similar difficulty. Did locals conceive of the three Mother Goddesses in the form in which we see them at Housesteads (t.c.1:1:32)? Sadly, now these figures are headless and it is not at all clear what they held in their hands, although to judge from other surviving images (like the one from Cirencester, Gloucestershire: Plate 4.32) these were likely to be objects with fertility symbolism such as small animals, baskets of fruit or loaves. Their images owe a good deal to other classical representations of seated goddesses, but in the case of *Genii Cucullati* (Figure 4.6) there is an obvious influence of local dress as

× Did locals envisage their gods in these ways or by Roman interps?

× t.c. 1:1:32

69

their 'duffle-coats' are based on hooded British cloaks. In answer to the question about these images as an access route to local cult, I would conclude that they are useful and valid, as long as they are approached with caution and an awareness of just how deeply they may have been shaped by Roman influence. (And of course, this observation does not just relate to their artistic images: note the Latinized forms of names such as Maponus and Cocidius.)

Finally, there is a question of artistic style in the context of culture, identity and power, and particularly the value of classical conventions in relation to local styles. As you will recall from earlier parts of the course, the classical approach in Roman art was essentially inherited from Greek art of the fifth century BC and emphasized naturalism in proportion and perspective; it is less easy to define what can qualify as 'local style', but often it involves a more schematic, less naturalistic representation and an interest in linear patterning. Of course there are cases where a classical deity is shown in a classical style (such as the little Diana figure, probably imported to Britain: t.c.1:10:21), or a local deity shown in a non-classical image (such as the horned god from Maryport: Plate 4.33), but the point to stress here is that there is no *automatic* link between 'Roman' subjects and 'classical' style or between the 'local' equivalents. This will be obvious from looking back at illustrations you have considered here: the emphatically Roman reliefs of the Bridgeness slab (Plate 4.27) show rather a 'non-classical' conception of proportion and perspective, while in contrast some native mother goddess images are quite classical in style. So the use of a particular style should not be read as an immediate expression of a particular power structure, but it may, as we have seen, offer some useful insights into cultural appropriation and aspects of identity. This is a topic you will consider further in a North African context in Block Five as it is an important theme in Roman provincial culture.

Part Four: Presenting Roman Britain

BY JANET HUSKINSON

In this last part of the block you will be looking at the question of presentation, that is, how events and people are represented in images which aim to elicit particular responses from viewers or readers. As you had cause to note in your work in the Introduction to the Course (particularly in Essays One and Two – remember the complexities of Philoppapus' self-representation), representation is a central part of communicating cultural values. The material you are going to study here illustrates just that. It comprises some ancient representations, first of Britannia and secondly of Boudicca, and then looks at how such themes are treated in more modern contexts, ending with some contemporary museum displays. It will also look at the role of gender in ancient constructions of social identity, since this is particularly relevant to the female personification and to the 'British queen'.

Your work in this section will involve listening to a talk on audio cassette (audio cassette 4, band 2), watching two sequences of video, reading from *Experiencing Rome* and the Supplementary Texts and referring to the Illustrations Book.

4.1 Event, image, and ideology

To start this section please look back at Plate 4.4 in the Illustrations Book, the sculpture from Aphrodisias, and at the scenario it presents.

Aphrodisias

Exercise

As you will remember, the exercise that you did on this image in the conclusion to Part One of the block showed how it set out a particular view of the Roman conquest of Britain in terms of culture, identity and power. This was an oppositional view that made the Romans into heroic conquerors who delivered the Britons a debilitating blow. (And you may also recall that this was the view of events repeatedly given in the passage you read by Goodman, pp.207–16.)

Romans heroic conquerors

But now you have worked on the event yourself and have looked closely at the source material; so what view have you arrived at? How far do you agree that the Roman conquest and local responses to it may be expressed in such clear-cut terms of two distinctive sides, victor and victim? Or are there other interpretations that can be made of the evidence?

victor/victim? other interps?

Discussion

Arguably the setting up of the *colonia* at Colchester and the circumstances surrounding the revolt of the Iceni in AD 60–61 could be interpreted in this way (as we shall see shortly), but most of the other historical evidence we have looked at suggests a much more nuanced view, as I suggested in my introduction to section 3.3. In fact almost everything you have worked on since reading the Goodman passage has indicated that the Roman conquest of Britain and local responses to it do not really fit in with such a polarized interpretation. You have seen evidence, for instance, that 'Roman' and 'Britons' were actually much more diverse categories than the sculpture suggests: 'Roman' soldiers came from all over the empire while the 'Britons' belonged to various groups with differing experiences of the occupation, and as you saw, there is evidence from sites along Hadrian's Wall for some two-way exchange of culture. So the historical situation seems to have been far more complex than this image implies.

This apparent mismatch is not simply because the Aphrodisias sculpture dates from an early stage in Britain's relationship with Rome: rather, it is because it is the nature of images to shape and present events according to some underlying idea. At Aphrodisias the ideology concerned the celebration of emperors and their achievements, and it is not surprising that this image of Claudius' conquest is couched in such terms. Nor is it surprising to find similar images continuing in other contexts where the motivating ideology was the advertisement of imperial power: think of the imagery used on many of the distance slabs from the Antonine Wall. Here too, on these later monuments, we find the same oppositional imagery being used to celebrate Roman triumph.

This brief exercise is a reminder of the gap that may exist between evidence which indicates 'life as lived' and other primary sources which set out a 'rhetorical' presentation of events from some particular ideological perspective. On the one hand, for instance, is the archaeological evidence to do with particular places (such as Camulodunum or Housesteads) or social groups (such as the women of Maryport, discussed in offprint 4.5, which has been included as optional reading). On the other are created images such as the Aphrodisias relief, where the historic event of the Roman conquest of Britain has been given this particular presentation in terms of classical heroism and a decisive end. Given that the sculpture was designed as one of a series decorating an imperial shrine, this slant is certainly not surprising. But it reminds us that historical events require presentation, even when they can be

Handwritten margin notes: no polarized interp / 'Roman', 'Briton' more diverse than victor/victim / 'Roman' soldiers all over emp[ire] / Buts belonged to various grps / Aphrodisia(s) — emperors + their achievements / distance slabs

reconstructed from observable fact, and that presentation inevitably involves a particular viewpoint and agenda. The figures used in representations like this (whether they are in the visual arts, as here, or in literature) play out these agenda, and their various roles are accentuated by other important factors, such as social background and status.

One such factor is gender, which in the Roman world was intimately related to concepts of social identity, and by this to relationships of power. As you have seen in the sculptures from Aphrodisias and the Antonine Wall, and in the various images of Britannia on Roman coins, gender is used in images as a way of articulating such relationships.

[handwritten margin note: gender social id. rel./power]

Exercise

In Essay Six, 'Reading gender in the Roman world', Dominic Montserrat describes gender in that context as 'a process of constantly renegotiated meanings which structured every aspect of Roman life' (p.164) in which masculine and feminine can be social constructions.

[handwritten margin note: Essay 6 gender]

What is crucial to note, and especially for the work you will be doing in the following sections, is that social role can be as important as biological sex in designating masculinity and femininity. The diagram at the start of Essay Six (p.154) is a useful way of visualizing the overlap between the two (i.e. the 'given' of biological sex and social role) which may of course be larger or smaller according to the specific social context. In other words, gender in the Roman world should be seen not as an essential condition, but one that is relative to setting and interpretation. (Essay One touched on this, and you may like to reread the relevant sections to refresh your memory about how such views fit into wider debates about identity.)

Please now read Essay Six.

4.2   Images of Boudicca

The theme of gender, and its social construction, carries into your work in this section: here you will be considering some of the issues involved in the representation of Boudicca by two ancient authors, Tacitus (in the *Annals* and the *Agricola*) and Cassius Dio. Boudicca led the British revolt against Rome in AD 60–61; if you want to remind yourself of the historical situation behind the revolt, look back at the end of Part Two of this block. (You will have a chance to look further at some other aspects of these accounts when you come to read Essay Ten on 'The language of dissent' in Block Five.)

Tacitus Dio Cassius not eyewitnesses

Parallel speeches

Tacitus Roman political agenda

Exercise

Tacitus' account of the revolt is given as extracts 4.3 and 4.4 and that of Cassius Dio is given as extract 4.5. Together these are rather long but just take them straight through as a 'good read', appreciating the dramatic action, paranormal portents, and set-piece speeches. (You have already read part of extract 4.3 in section 3.2 of this block.) Neither writer was of course an eye-witness, and Cassius Dio who wrote (in Greek) in the early third century seems to have drawn on Tacitus' accounts for his own. But above all it is important to remember once again the kind of literary and rhetorical traditions that shaped their writing so thoroughly. Here, for instance, we see the motif of parallel speeches created for the mouths of the Roman leader and the barbarian queen, like opposing sides in an oratorical debate, and Tacitus in particular makes constant allusions to the Roman political agenda of his own day (as David Braund showed in his discussion of Tacitus as a source for Britain in audio cassette 4, band 1).

Please read these extracts now, and as you read, focus on the question of gender and how it is used, explicitly and implicitly, to shape the presentation of people and events.

Discussion

As you will have noticed, gender is a theme which runs throughout the accounts of Tacitus and Cassius Dio. It seems that the fact that the barbarian protagonist was a woman has opened up a discourse about what is appropriate to women, and to men, in terms of appearance, social behaviour and morality. In this case we are considering not the veracity of the historical statements (such as: did Boudicca look like this? is this how British queens were expected to act? and so on), but how these issues are presented within these literary accounts of the event.

Tacitus

Tacitus (extract 4.3, paragraph 35) lets Boudicca herself say that the Britons were used to women leaders, and imply that while British men might prefer to settle for enslavement at the end of the day, hers would be a nobler fate. In fact according to Tacitus (extract 4.3, paragraph 37) she kills herself in defeat (while Cassius Dio has her die, presumably of natural causes). Her suicide in honourable defeat is paralleled by that of the Roman Poenius Postumus who was dishonoured in the victory by his earlier refusal to take forces to his colleagues. Perhaps even less honourable is the action of the Roman official Catus Decianus who flees to Gaul to escape the consequences of his actions (extract 4.3, paragraph 32).

If the Britons were used to women as leaders (though Tacitus shows at paragraph 33 of extract 4.3 that not all women went to war), Romans, according to this rhetoric, despised them. They abused their women prisoners, including Boudicca and her daughters (though the Britons were also merciless to enemy women: see Cassius Dio, extract 4.5, paragraph 7), and despised them as adversaries (Tacitus, extract 4.3, paragraph 36). As Cassius Dio comments, the whole disaster had an extra shame for the Romans since it was inflicted by a woman; but as you may have noticed, he softens the horror of this by allowing her to be an exceptional woman in terms of spirit and looks (a tall warrior figure, in fact rather like a man, though Cassius Dio does not explicitly say so). Tacitus on the other hand is at pains (extract 4.3, paragraph 35) to emphasize the fact that she participates in the fight to avenge the Roman crimes against humanity and not to fight as a queen.

[handwritten margin notes: Cassius Dio - shame on Romans to Boudicca a woman - on exceptional tho' - like a man. Tacitus - Boudicca fighting Romans for humanitarian reasons]

Exercise

Now that you have identified for yourself some aspects of gender as a theme in these descriptions, please listen to audio cassette 4, band 2 as David Braund discusses each of these literary portraits of Boudicca, looking at how it has been carefully constructed by the writer, and why.

Braund discusses Tacitus, *Annals* (extract 4.3), the *Agricola* (extract 4.4) and Cassius Dio (extract 4.5) in order, so you will need to have your Supplementary Texts ready and open, and may like to stop and restart the tape as you work through what he says.

[handwritten margin note: Braund]

For each case, note down:

1   what Braund identifies as features of the overall context in which the writer is setting his presentation of Boudicca;

2   what aspects of Boudicca and her situation he consequently presents;

3   any particular words or themes he employs in order to do this.

Discussion

As you heard, Braund shows in each case that the author has chosen significant words, or selected particular events, to shape his image of Boudicca. The key points to have in your answers may be summed up as follows.

[handwritten margin note: Significant words & phrases to shape image of Boudicca]

First, for the *Annals* (extract 4.3):

1   The wider contextualizing themes are to do with justice and the proper practices of an ordered society (for example, the wills,

Civilization v barbarity

Contemp. pol. concerns at Rome - opposition gender politics

and the theme of liberty and servitude you met in audio cassette 4, band 1), and conversely, the abuse of such procedures and its inevitable violent consequences. Related to these are ideas about what constitutes civilization and barbarity (for instance, the acquisition of reason and self-control, summed up in the Latin word *ratio* which Braund quotes, as opposed to the simple natural disposition of a 'noble savage'). Braund also picks up on two themes to do with contemporary political concerns at Rome: first, how to deal with being in opposition (you can find the case of Thrasea Paetus that Braund cites in Tacitus, *Annals* 14, paragraphs 48–9), and second (as he mentions later in contrast to the *Agricola*), gender politics at the capital, which are also discussed elsewhere in *Annals* 14.

Boudicca sympathetic victim - avenge - a wife, not queen

barbarian :- not able to think things thro'

her speech based on emotion

Tacitus believed better one's time to oppose tyranny

2 Given these concerns, Tacitus presents Boudicca as a sympathetic victim of all this, who seeks to avenge the wrongs inflicted on her, her family and her people. He is careful to point out that she is not a queen but a wife (the Latin word *uxor*, quoted by Braund), wronged by 'the worst parts of Roman imperialism'. Her opposition is justified, yet as Braund explains, it was doomed to fail because she was a barbarian and therefore unable 'to think things through'. Her speech, as Tacitus words it (paragraph 35), is based on emotion rather than on careful strategic thinking. It urges the kind of precipitate action that contrasted with Tacitus' own belief that effective opposition to tyranny might involve biding one's time.

Tacitus minimizes 'native' element - Boudicca - dignified woman - Brits used to woman leaders

3 One way in which Tacitus seems to link these Roman political themes into this obviously British scenario is to minimize the 'native' element in his portrayal of Boudicca herself. In the brief vignettes in paragraphs 31, 35 and 37 she appears very much as a dignified woman, couched in terms that are quite Roman: as Braund points out she even has to explain to her troops – and so to the Roman audience – that in Britain it was quite usual for women to be leading the battle. Her actions, though in this case perhaps unexpected by Romans, uphold rather than transgress social norms for a woman.

Tacitus stresses Roman violence excessive

To heighten his presentation of Boudicca as victim, Tacitus stresses the uncontrolled and excessive nature of Roman violence: this again raises questions about who is 'civilized' and who is not in these events.

Secondly, the *Agricola* (extract 4.4):

1 The brevity of this passage and reference to Boudicca is very much related to the overall purpose of the *Agricola*, which as you

will remember from Part One of this block, was primarily concerned with the life of Agricola, and, underlying that with questions about how best to govern a place such as Britain. Tactics, especially in terms of how best to treat the natives, are a central question. And even in this brief extract you will notice the theme of servitude (*servitium*), symbolized by the *colonia* at Colchester (just as in the *Annals* 14, paragraph 31, Tacitus described its temple of Claudius as 'a stronghold of eternal tyranny').

2   In consequence Boudicca herself is scarcely characterized, beyond being a female leader (*femina duce*, as Braund quotes). She is not a victim: on the contrary under her leadership the Britons extracted a cruel and effective revenge.

3   Here, too, there is little to note except perhaps how Tacitus evokes the savage cruelty this time inflicted by the Britons.

Finally, Cassius Dio (extract 4.5):

1   As Braund points out, Cassius Dio in his time shared many of Tacitus' views, seeing Rome's empire from a senatorial perspective. He too emphasizes Roman mismanagement, especially through financial exploitation amongst the causes of the British revolt. (Look back at the end of Part Two if you want to remind yourself of some of this.) As you have just seen for yourself, he draws on gender issues as a powerful way of criticizing abuses of power in Nero's Rome.

2   Boudicca, in consequence, is presented rather as an antithesis to Roman expectations of womanly behaviour; but this is scarcely surprising as Cassius Dio describes her as a barbarian queen – a position which would seem doubly threatening to many conventionally-thinking Romans. The rather masculine characteristics she is assigned allow her to be contrasted with the weak and effeminate (and therefore powerless) Nero, who in turn is contrasted with other Roman imperial women, Messalina and Agrippina, who, trangressively, took power in Rome. So here the gender imagery is used very vividly in connection with identity and power, and Boudicca is placed at the centre of this.

3   To this end Cassius Dio uses equally vivid language: as Braund says he paints her as a 'monstrous', frightening figure. She is like a man, not just in physical appearance but in spirit (paragraph 2). She communes with strange (that is, non-Roman deities, female too), and has supernatural powers, symbolized by the

highly rhetorical speeches
hard, simple living Brits v. soft degenerate life' Rome

compare luxura from Greece

hare. The speeches that Cassius Dio puts into her mouth are highly rhetorical in construction and sentiment, and contain a lot of imagery contrasting hard, simple-living Britons with the soft, degenerate life of Rome. (You may recognize some of these themes and language from the similar kind of things said in the debate about the effects of *luxuria* imported from Greece that you considered for Roman Italy in Block Two, section 3.1.)

exercise caution re ref. B. to ancient writers

In discussing these portraits Braund reminds us that it is all too easy to think of a composite 'Boudicca', combined from all these different *ancient* accounts. Some of his comments about this obviously tie in with the warning he gave on the earlier band (audio cassette 4, band 1) about taking excerpts from Tacitus without reference to their wider context. It is important to exercise such caution when we are looking at how Boudicca was represented by these ancient writers, and why.

But in the topic we turn to now, the composite picture is prominent; and what is more, it is remade over and over again as, in response to the needs of their own culture and society, different generations engage with the figure of Boudicca.

4.3 Images of Boadicea

'reception'
Aug. Rome poets + writers drew on model from Greece to express past values - own culture
Mussolini adopted Aug. images of power + empire

This process of adaptation of themes and images from the past by later cultures is often known in scholarly terms as 'reception'. You have already met it in the course, for instance in Block One when poets and artists in Augustan Rome drew on images from Greece to express the particular values of their own culture, or when Augustan images of power and empire were in their turn adopted by Mussolini for twentieth-century political ends.

As you will see even from just comparing the titles of this section and the last, the change from ancient to post-classical persona is marked in this case by a shift of name: the Boudicca of ancient sources (spelled sometimes with a single 'c') becomes the later Boadicea. This 'new' name seems to have come about through a series of changes that occurred in the transmission of texts (some perhaps mistakes), but it serves as a useful way of distinguishing the classical figure from her later version. And as you will see now this later version is multifarious, truly a 'phenomenon'.

Exercise

VC2

The interview with Carolyn Williams on 'The Boadicea phenomenon' (video cassette 2, sequence 4; t.c.1:19:10–1:40:41) looks at later images of Boadicea down to the present day.

Watch this interview now, and as you do so, ask yourself the following questions.

Which details of the ancient literary portraits of Boudicca are used in these later images of Boadicea?

Which of her ancient roles (e.g. mother, leader) are repeated, and for what particular causes?

Which images are described here as 'ambiguous', or 'double-edged', and why?

And finally, what about you as a viewer? What do you bring to these images in terms of your own expectations? How did your image of Boadicea come about?

(At one point, Cowper's poem, *Ode to Boadicea* is discussed; the full text of the poem is reproduced as extract 4.7.)

Discussion

Obviously no one can answer the last questions but you! Yet whatever your responses were, they are intimately connected with the versatility of Boadicea as a symbolic figure, which Carolyn Williams emphasizes in her vivid selection of examples for this interview. As you have seen, Boadicea was adopted to represent many different causes over time – 'imperialist icon', 'champion of militant feminism', 'the rebel in the soul', and a 'powerful woman who breaks moulds' are some of the phrases used in the interview to describe her. It is obvious too that most of these images show strong derivation from the classical versions, either in the graphic details they pick out (the hare, for example; t.c.1:23:43), or in developing particular roles for Boadicea. Some draw on the wronged wife and mother of Tacitus' *Annals*, 'a decent woman' as David Braund described her, while others (such as the Toyah Wilcox version: t.c.1:26:38) are closer to Cassius Dio's frightening figure. Both the private and public aspects of her life are represented with equal prominence, and it is particularly interesting when the two get merged. An example of this is in the Suffragist drawing you saw at the end (t.c.1:37:52) which showed Boadicea as mother and leader, alongside images of contemporary mothers and daughters.

Given the multiplicity of roles she can play – as victim, as woman, as rebel fighting against social injustice, as 'insider' and 'outsider' – it is not surprising that on occasions she becomes an ambiguous figure. Thornycroft's statue is a case in point: does it represent Boadicea as an endorsement of the Establishment, or as a rebel against it? Or does it want to play with both ideas simultaneously?

How can we tell? In images like these where several ideas seem to be presented simultaneously the viewer's own expectations become very important, and this is the point of the questions about your own personal image of Boadicea. Even if you have never thought much about her before, the fact is that you inevitably bring something of your own ideas to your reading of these images, and this will be a central factor in the meaning you give to such 'open' images. For as we have clearly seen, the figure of Boadicea has no single significance, fixed for all time, but is re-invented, as it were, with a value relative to changing circumstances. She can be whatever we need to make of her, either in forming our own image, or in interpreting those of others; this makes our role as viewer (or reader) a central one. (This point will come up again in the final section of this block in the discussion of museum displays.)

To sum up for now, certain points emerge from this interview that are important for the work which you will now go on to do in the final section of this block. First, figures and events from the past can be interpreted and re-interpreted according to the cultural interests of new generations and new societies. Second, in this process the ideological standpoint of the interpreter and presenter is crucial: it reshapes the image, selecting the new values it is to carry. Third, the viewer also has a powerful role in this, especially on occasions where the image offers a number of potential readings: he or she can make the choice.

4.4   Presenting the past: 'fact' and 'fiction'

The reception of Boadicea in post-classical art and literature involved, as you have seen, a wide variety of artistic media and cultural contexts. It is not difficult to appreciate the creative imagination that inspired many of these representations. This is also the case with many films, books and plays set in Roman times, from Shakespeare's *Julius Caesar* to *Ben Hur*, from *I, Claudius* to *Up Pompeii*; and in approaching the view of Roman history that they offer we are usually quite aware of how it has been shaped by the particular aims and purpose of the presentation, and as readers or viewers we react to it according to our expectations of 'fiction'. But what of presentations which we expect to deal in 'fact'? History books, television documentaries and museum displays all present situations in which we often assume that we will find the past presented in a straightforward, 'objective' way – and that is often despite the fact that our studies have made us quick to spot the biases of ancient historians and artists! But it is an obvious fact that all these forms of presenting the past are constructs involving the selection and setting out of material on the basis of certain ideas. As they are also concerned to communicate these ideas about the past, the reader or viewer has a further important part to play.

In the next block you will consider some of these issues and how they have affected the presentation of Roman archaeology in North Africa: and in the next video sequence of this block, you will be looking at the display of Romano-British material in museum collections and at some of the ideas and implications that are involved.

But before you move to this final video and the specific questions it will raise, I want to draw together some of the issues that have emerged so far in this discussion as important themes and factors in the representation of the historical past. Many, but not all, of them will emerge again in looking at the museum collections.

As you have already seen (in images of Britannia and Boudicca/Boadicea), gender, ethnicity and national culture often play a central part in the representation of the past, in terms of ideas and their artistic formulation. As you will remember from Essays One and Six, questions about gender and ethnicity are often to do with how far these are fixed and given elements, and how far they may be negotiated or shaped up by other elements in the cultural context: are people characterized as 'female' or 'barbarian' to marginalize them? (Or alternatively, does 'male' usually equate with the powerful 'insider'?) Does the representation take the insider's or outsider's point of view? You have already had occasion to ask yourself questions like these, in the various representations of Boudicca/Boadicea, and they are important too for evaluating the material in this next video sequence.

Nationalism and a sense of nationhood are concepts which were not discussed in Essay One, since they do not really arise in the ancient world (beyond, perhaps, attachment to the city-state); the idea of the 'nation state' belongs to more modern history. But they are often influential in the presentation of the past. Where the 'nation' is also a ruling 'empire', as Britain has been, then the imperial past of Rome offers some powerful resonances and points of reference, as can be seen from many instances in the arts and scholarship of Britain in the second half of the nineteenth and the earlier twentieth centuries. Through evoking the experiences of the Roman empire, the British were able to consider their own experiences of empire, and to suggest some line of cultural continuity between the two. You have already seen a little of how Kipling imagined the Roman experience in Britain as a theme for historical adventure (extract 4.6). An even more potent illustration is Joseph Conrad's novel, *Heart of Darkness* (published in 1899). In the passage given as extract 4.8, the narrator prefaces his own experiences travelling up the Congo as an agent of a colonial company with musings about what a Roman may have felt as he embarked on his imperialist enterprise at the Thames. In scholarship, this was the period in which the concept of Romanization was developed primarily in the work of Francis Haverfield, who delivered a lecture entitled 'The Romanization of Britain' to the British Academy in 1905 (expanded into a book in 1912). He 'visualized Romanization as directional and progressive, the process by which native social groups in Roman Britain became increasingly "Roman" ', a process with 'positive moral content' (Hingley, 1966, p.39).

But for Britain this historical model was somewhat paradoxical and double-edged, since it had itself been subjected to conquest by the Romans. This opened up two possibilities for later British identification with the lot of their forebears. One was to cast them as freedom-fighters resisting domination. The other was to show how Britons under Roman guidance had acquired the civilizing arts and technology which enabled them to become in turn, centuries later, the beneficent instructors of their own subject peoples. The painting reproduced as Plate 4.34, 'Building the Roman Wall', was one of a series painted for Wallington Hall near Newcastle upon Tyne, a series which finishes with a picture celebrating the Victorian industrial revolution; here local Britons are shown labouring under the benign control of Roman masters. It has been observed (by Smiles, 1994, p.147) that the picture shows a marked difference in the physiognomies of the 'superior' Roman and the 'primitive' Britons: this will be familiar to you from the similar contrast made on the Roman tombstone which shows the soldier Longinus and his British victim (Plate 4.18). Other contemporary images were equally explicit: the series described in offprint 4.6 juxtaposed Britain's ancient past with her imperial present to make a clear message about the redemptive nature of imperialism. But in other cases the precise nature of the historical reference is less clear, and the image offers a variety of possible readings. This is illustrated well by some of the later images of Boadicea (Thornycroft's statue, for instance; t.c.1:31:27). They also show just how important it is to think about the standpoint taken by the representation: is it showing a 'Roman' experience (of victory, of empire, with its mission to civilize and pacify, for instance), or the view of the conquered, dispossessed, and marginalized? Or does it perhaps manage to represent both views at once? These are questions which clearly apply to the presentation of some of the museum material that you will see in the next video sequence.

You will next watch video cassette 2, sequence 5. You have already met some of the monuments mentioned in the sequence and may find the following cross-references useful:

the temple of Claudius, Colchester: Block Four, section 2.3; Plate 4.14; extract 4.3, paragraph 31;

the Stanway burials: Block Four, section 2.2;

the tomb of Classicianus: Block Four, section 1.2; Figure 4.1; extract 4.3, paragraph 38;

the Longinus tombstone, Colchester: Block Four, section 3.2; Plate 4.18.

Classis Britannica: this inscription from the fort at Benwell mentioned at t.c.1:47:43 is fragmentary, but the wording is restored as *classis Britannica*, referring to the British fleet, because this is known to have been involved in construction work on Hadrian's Wall.

Exercise

As you watch video cassette 2, sequence 5, 'Presenting Roman Britain' (t.c.1:40:48–1:57:52), please think about how you would answer these questions.

1   How have the different museums addressed the changes which have occurred in historical perspectives over the last decades (for instance, away from imperial history)?

2   How far is an element of interpretation inevitable in any presentation of the past, whether in museum displays or on video?

Discussion

1   The question of changing historical perspectives underlies many of the discussions in this video sequence, although there is explicit mention of major shifts from imperial and military history towards an interest in gender and native cultures. Addressing these involves both a new look at the available material evidence (by finding artefacts in the collections that might illustrate these topics), and reassessment of the values hitherto given to the historical events or movements which generated it (by reconsidering the Romans as the force of occupation, or the lives of women and children, for instance).

As you will have seen and heard here, museums vary in their response to this challenge and, interestingly, for various reasons. If we look more closely at the factors which conditioned their response, we get an insight into the range of attitudes and practicalities which so often combine to shape a museum's presentation of the past. One immediate factor is the nature of the material in the collection. A national museum such as the British Museum is likely to have a much larger collection of objects from which it can select in response to new interests than have many regional museums which are more immediately dependent on what their locality has yielded. As Lindsay Allason-Jones commented (t.c.1:50:27), the native population in the north does not seem to have had a material culture which has survived in the local archaeological record; but Colchester is able to demonstrate the wealth of the British élites through their burials at Stanway (t.c.1:44:25). Furthermore, the original basis of a collection may have resulted in its having a particular bias: nineteenth-century antiquarians interested in the Romans and in classical culture would tend to concentrate on the Roman side of things, as can be seen at Chesters, for instance (starting at t.c.1:45:05). In terms of display, this museum is in itself an illustration of changing historical perspectives: by keeping to its original style of presentation, within its early twentieth-century building, Chesters presents itself as a piece of our own recent cultural history. Colchester too exploits the Roman history of its building, but overall has a very different approach to updating its presentations and making them interactive for the visitor (the medieval music in the background while Peter Berridge spoke at t.c.1:43:20 had drifted across from a later period gallery).

Another major factor in a museum's response to changing historical interests is likely to be its own policy towards interpreting its material for the visitor, which will be discussed more fully below. Where overt interpretation is part of a policy of presentation, then the museum's response to change is likely to be more obvious: information displays, labelling and guidebooks will all promote the new viewpoints to reinforce the message of the artefacts themselves. In contrast, a museum which has not the scope for or interest in large-scale interpretation, may approach the matter of change rather differently: at Newcastle upon Tyne, as you heard (t.c.1:53:41), the material and its presentation has stayed more or less the same but 'people's attitude to it has changed as they go along'.

2   The importance of 'people's attitude' becomes apparent again when we consider whether interpretation is to some degree inevitable in presenting the past. In the video sequence on archaeology at Arbeia you saw how material excavated at the site was then carefully recorded and classified according to objective criteria about its date or type, for instance; and one might reasonably expect that a similar approach could be sustained when the material reaches the museum displays. So is interpretation really inevitable? At Colchester it was made clear that they had taken a deliberate decision to offer a particular

interpretation. Chesters, by contrast, simply identifies the objects. But even this presentation is not without selectivity and interpretation. Presumably the antiquarians collecting material from sites on Hadrian's Wall were ultimately selective, while the style of display expects visitors to supply questions and answers about the objects for themselves. It is a reminder that in every display there are contributions to be made by both presenter and the visitor, and that neither of these can be completely free of value judgement. Presentation inevitably involves some selection, of the objects to be shown, or of the way in which they are to be physically arranged in the display or described in labels and guidebooks. Visitors, too, bring expectations and prejudices even if they come with open minds to pick up new knowledge about the objects on display, and this is a major and inevitable factor in creating new interpretations.

Of course, it will not have escaped you that most of these points can be applied to this video which is another way of presenting the past! Here, too, there has been editing and selection, from the particular historical situation of the late 1990s. In selecting the material for this video, *I* have been taking one particular line and using some practical opportunities to interview staff at museums which we were already visiting. (You will have already studied some of the material in earlier video sequences in this block.) The producer, Mags Noble, then worked with me to interpret the ideas through this visual medium, shaping up the relationship between script and image, since some points are better made through words and others through pictures. The video editor, Denise Taylor, edited the material we had recorded to maximize its effectiveness as a visual argument: an illustration of the kind of choices she made is the juxtaposition of the heads of Claudius and Antenociticus at t.c.1:50:18–20 to evoke the 'impact of Roman culture on the native population' specifically mentioned in my commentary. So here as in the museum presentation there is a range of reasons behind the editing process, from the technical to the ideological and academic; however even-handed I intended my approach to be, it has necessarily been shaped and constrained by all these further considerations. Another related question is how we have approached the issue of identifying the items which we have presented on the video (in other words, how we are 'labelling' our 'exhibits'). The answer is that in the Course Guide we have produced a list of the pieces which gives relevant details about them, so you can follow them up further if you wish.

And then there is *your* position as viewer and reader: how far is your interpretation of these facets of Roman Britain shaped by your own situation? As the video suggested, your own geographical origins may be an important factor. Perhaps if you come from Colchester or northern Scotland you have strong views about Roman occupation and British reactions to it; or you may see the Roman empire in a particular light if your own family originated from a country colonized by a modern empire. Of course, you will have your own answers to all this, but the point of the question is to heighten awareness of the different roles involved in the representation of the past, where the viewers and the experiences they bring inevitably interact with the image that is being offered.

Conclusion to Block Four

Although the focus chosen for this block on Roman Britain was (deliberately) small – the impact of Roman military conquest as seen in certain times and places – the range of issues directly connected with the course themes of culture, identity, and power has been wide. This becomes very clear if you look back over the ground you have covered in this block from two particular angles.

The first involves the work you did on the sources. This showed that a powerful factor in their creation and interpretation is the cultural identity of the various people involved, ancient authors, modern presenters (interpreting material on sites, or presenting artefacts to the public in museums), and viewers and readers with their own important part in creating meaning. It was a reminder that representation is a central process in communicating the shared values of any culture, and the 'Boadicea phenomenon' showed how images may be reworked over a long period of time to respond to changes in those values.

The second angle is the historical material itself. Much of this was to do with cultural change that took place in communities or in 'frontier zones', with the impact of the Roman invading power. This material contained some important questions, particularly to do with the nature and extent of change, and with its processes. As you will have realized by now, these are the kinds of questions to which there are no easy answers, but they will go on being hotly debated by archaeologists and historians from their views of the evidence: Roman Britain is fertile ground for the Romanization debate (look back to Essay One if you want to remind yourself of the issues involved in that). The final point to be made concerns identity: several topics you have studied here have shown again how social identity is a complex matter. It is potentially multi-facetted (that is to say that people define themselves, and others, in several simultaneous ways), and it is relative to situations. Male, female, 'Roman', 'Briton' are categories which are not essentially fixed, but may be dependent on certain social roles and behaviour: thus Longinus from Bulgaria can be styled a Roman soldier in his memorial, and barbarian Boudicca can be seen as acting with greater civility and manliness than her Roman opponents.

If I had to choose a single word to sum up these themes as they have emerged in looking at Britain, it would be 'plurality'. You may like to carry this over as a point to test out against the material that you will meet as you turn now to look at a rather different part of the empire, Roman North Africa.

Key dates

BC	55/54	Julius Caesar's expeditions to Britain
	?34, ?27, ?26	Augustus' planned expeditions to Britain
AD	43	Claudius' invasion of Britain
	43–47	Aulus Plautius governor of Britain
	44	Building of the legionary fort at Colchester
	49	Foundation of the *colonia* at Colchester
	54	Death of Claudius; accession of Nero
	60–61	Revolt of the Iceni against the Romans led by Boudicca; Colchester, London, Verulamium sacked
	78 to *c.* 84	Agricola's campaigns in eastern Scotland, culminating in Roman victory at 'Mons Graupius' in *c.* 84
	from *c.* 87–100	Roman withdrawal from Scotland, to Tyne–Solway line
	122	Hadrian visits Britain; building of Hadrian's Wall commenced
	140–*c.* 142	Antonine conquests in southern Scotland; building of Antonine Wall between the Forth and Clyde
	by 163	Antonine Wall finally abandoned; new building work at Hadrian's Wall
	208–211	Campaigns of Septimius Severus and Caracalla in Scotland
	211	Death of Septimius Severus in York

References

BOWMAN, A.K. and THOMAS, J.D. (1983) *Vindolanda: The Latin Writing Tablets*, Britannia Monograph Series 4, London, Society for the Promotion of Roman Studies.

BOWMAN, A.K. and THOMAS, J.D. (1994) *The Vindolanda Writing Tablets (Tabulae Vindolandenses II)*, London, British Museum Press.

COLLINGWOOD, R.G. and WRIGHT, R.P. (eds) (1995, second edition) *The Roman Inscriptions of Britain*, Stroud, Alan Sutton Publishing (first published 1965).

CRUMMY, P. (1997) *City of Victory: the Story of Colchester – Britain's First Roman Town*, Colchester, Colchester Archaeological Trust.

DOBSON, B. and MANN, J.C. (1973) 'The Roman army in Britain and Britons in the Roman Army', *Britannia*, vol.4, pp.191–205.

HINGLEY, R. (1996) 'The 'legacy' of Rome: the ride, decline and fall of the theory of Romanization' in J. Webster and N.J. Cooper (eds) *Roman Imperialism: Post-colonial Perspectives*, Leicester Archaeological Monographs no.3, pp.35–48.

HOLDER, P.A. (1982) *The Roman Army in Britain*, London, Batsford.

JAMES S. and RIGBY, V. (1997) *Britain and the Celtic Iron Age*, London, British Museum Press.

MACMULLEN, R. (1984) 'The Legion as a society', *Historia*, vol.33, pp.440–56.

MILLETT, M. (1990) *The Romanization of Britain*, Cambridge, Cambridge University Press.

MILLETT, M. (1995) *Roman Britain*, London, English Heritage/Batsford.

SALLER, R. and SHAW, B. (1984) 'Tombstones and Roman family relations in the Principate: civilians, soldiers and slaves', *Journal of Roman Studies*, vol.84, pp.124–56.

SALWAY, P. (1993) *The Oxford Illustrated History of Britain*, Oxford, Oxford University Press.

SALWAY, P. (1997) *A History of Roman Britain*, Oxford, Oxford University Press.

SMILES, S. (1994) *The Image of Antiquity: Ancient Britain and the Romantic Imagination*, New Haven, Yale University Press.

SMITH, R.R.R. (1987) 'The imperial reliefs from the Sebasteion at Aphrodisias', *Journal of Roman Studies*, vol.77, pp.88–138.

SMITH, R.R.R. (1988) '*Simulacra gentium*: the Ethne from the Sebasteion at Aphrodisias', *Journal of Roman Studies*, vol.78, pp.50–77.

Further reading

None of the following books are part of the essential reading for the course, but are suggested as places where you may like to follow up specific topics of interest to you.

ALLASON-JONES, L. (1989) *Women in Roman Britain*, London, British Museum Press.

BÉDOYÈRE, G. DE LA (1999) *Companion to Roman Britain*, Stroud, Tempus.

BOWMAN, A.K. (1994) *Life and Letters on the Roman Frontier: Vindolanda and its People*, London, British Museum Press.

BRAUND, D. (1996) *Ruling Roman Britain: Kings, Queens, Governors and Emperors from Julius Caesar to Agricola*, London, Routledge.

BREEZE, D.J. and DOBSON, B. (1991) *Hadrian's Wall*, Harmondsworth, Penguin.

HENIG, M. (1984) *Religion in Roman Britain*, London, Batsford.

HOLDER, P.A. (1982) *The Roman Army in Britain*, London, Batsford.

IRELAND, S. (1996) *Roman Britain: A Sourcebook*, second edition, London, Routledge.

KEPPIE L. (1998) *Roman Inscribed and Sculptured Stones in the Hunterian Museum, University of Glasgow*, London, Society for the Promotion of Roman Studies.

KEPPIE L. (1998) *Scotland's Roman Remains*, second edition, Edinburgh, John Donald.

SHOTTER, D. (1996) *The Roman Frontier in Britain*, Preston, Carnegie Publishing.

WILSON, R.J.A (1996) *A Guide to the Roman Remains of Britain*, third edition, London, Constable.

WYKE, M. (1997) *Projecting the Past: Ancient Rome, Cinema and History*, London, Routledge.